Front cover

Beating Across the Golden Gate, Master Mariners' Race, July 4, 1884 ...
*The three-masted lumber schooner, Occidental and two scow schooners
moving on a fresh westerly that cost one of the Occidental's crew a broken
wrist as he tried to muzzle the topsail's blowing out. The crowds lining the
wharves and Telegraph Hill could see the start of the race at the foot of Market
Street and catch the middle and the finish from Fort Point, past Telegraph
Hill and home.*

William Letts Oliver photograph,
National Maritime Museum,
San Francisco

SCHOONERS OF
SAN FRANCISCO BAY

BY ROGER R. OLMSTED

as edited by NANCY OLMSTED
with a foreword by KARL KORTUM

*Two men, some scow . . .
A point in time . . .
A place in space . . .*

CALIFORNIA HISTORY CENTER

Local History Studies Volume 33   Cupertino, California

Sponsored by a grant from the National Maritime Association
at San Francisco.

Edited by Nancy Olmsted.
Managing editor, N. Kathleen Peregrin.
Executive editor, James C. Williams.

10 9 8 7 6 5 4 3 2 1

First Edition

Library of Congress Cataloging-in-Publication Data

Olmsted, Roger R., 1927-1981.
    Scow schooners of San Francisco Bay by Roger R. Olmsted;
as edited by Nancy Olmsted; with a foreword by Karl Kortum.
— 1st ed. p. 112, 21.6 cm. — (Local history studies, ISSN
0276-4105; v. 33)
    Bibliography: p. 97.
    Includes index.
    ISBN 0-935089-12-8
    1. Scow schooners — California — San Francisco Bay Area
— History.
2. Shipping — California — San Francisco Bay Area — History.
I. Olmsted, Nancy L. II. Title. III. Series.
VM311.F7046 1988
387.2'26'097946—dc19

                        88-14463
                          CIP

Contents

National Maritime Museum
San Francisco

The Turn of the Century Remained Vivid in the 1950s . . . *Roger R. Olmsted realized that the recollections of mariners were as important to collect as the last of the ships they sailed. Men in their 60s and 70s had become the* *last working mariners from the age of sail. He took them seriously as professional sailors and he enjoyed tracking them down to document their lives.*

Foreword

In the 1950s a witty and outrageous intellectual by the name of Roger Olmsted hove over the Maritime Museum's horizon. He was a fifth generation San Franciscan who had grown up handling his father's sailboat on the bay. He never was happier than when looking at boats, talking about boats, or talking with the men who sailed them. At the University of California, where he was commodore of the yacht club, he appropriately sailed a Jolly Boat designed by England's Uffa Fox. Later he sailed a Swedish canoe that had a revolving mast and out-rigger seats for wet rides across San Francisco Bay.

At seventeen Roger had appointments to West Point and Annapolis. Sworn in at the naval academy, and so handsome that this event appeared on the cover of *Life* magazine, the northern Californian was dismayed to find himself starting down the path of a military career that had little to do with ships that sail. He resigned his appointment and headed for the University of Nevada.

I met him about this time and suggested the scow schooners of San Francisco Bay as a subject worthy of his thesis. As a museum director from the river port of Petaluma, where the *Alma* still came with oyster shell and the *Matilda* had shortly before left off cargo carrying, I long had felt that this definitive craft needed a chronicler. The work that resulted was scholarly in scope and detail but also highly readable. It included splendid anecdotes from that vanishing breed in the 1950s, the scow schooner men.

Roger's efforts came in the nick of time. He was able to interview Emil Munder and H. S. Thomsen, the scow schooner builders at Hunter's Point. He wrote an account that could not possibly be duplicated today, and it is now published for the first time. Some 400 scow schooners finally had a celebrant. And a brilliant one.

On the strength of this work I asked Roger to become Curator of the San Francisco Maritime Museum. He immersed himself in the William Letts Oliver photographs of the Master Mariner's Race in 1884, as that discerning but offhand Oakland collector, J. Porter Shaw, had preserved the glass negatives in a box under his workbench. Many of these fine photographs and Roger's description of the 1884 regatta are included in *Scow Schooners of San Francisco Bay*. The article he wrote and illustrated with these pictures for *Yachting* and *American West* revived interest in this forgotten race so that it is now again a fixture on San Francisco Bay.

As museum curator Roger applied his finely-honed intelligence to a wide range of problems, from creating cataloging codes to applied seamanship — solutions still in use three decades later. For example, he created a coded subject filing method for the museum's burgeoning photographic collection. A lobbying effort by the museum persuaded the State of California to purchase historic ships with tideland oil royalties. Roger swarmed all over this program in useful ways. He researched individual ships, such as the lumber schooner, *C. A. Thayer*, and produced volumes to implement their restoration and display at San Francisco's Hyde Street Pier.

But perhaps Roger's greatest skill lay in his ability to conceive of imaginative research and publishing projects and then carry them out with the attention to exquisite detail that marks the artist. After he left the museum, his choice, Roger

The 1950 rescue of **Ada Iredale**, *ca. 1872 . . . A lady with a lively past is pried loose from her cement base in the Marin garden of Captain Saunders, Captain Matson's Marine Superintendent.*

Ada Iredale *was an iron ship built in Harrington, England in 1872, which caught on fire 1900 miles east of the Marquesas Islands while carrying a load of coal. Abandoned by her crew she drifted as a smoldering derelict in the Pacific for almost a year before being rescued by a French man o'war and towed into Papeete. Captain I. E. Thayer of San Francisco put out her fire, patched up her plates and brought her home. As the* Annie Johnson *she sailed as one of Matson's first seven ships.*

Rescued from a fate worse than death, her figurehead now resides in the National Maritime Museum at San Francisco.

Both views, Karl Kortum, National Maritime Museum, San Francisco

Roger Olmsted and Walter Taylor on board one of the derelict scows in the 1950s . . . They examine the center-board well of an unknown scow sloop, rotting on the mud of Corte Madera Creek in Marin County.

set a new standard for local architectural history when he wrote (with his friend Tom Watkins) *Here Today: San Francisco's Architectural History*, based on original research by San Francisco's Junior League. From 1973 until the time of his death in 1981, he produced nine major studies on San Francisco's historical archaeological resources. One of these thick volumes, *San Francisco Waterfront* (1976), an enormously useful work, became a model for cultural resource documents that were publishable as social histories. His book *Mirror of the Dream*, an illustrated history of San Francisco, co-authored with Tom Watkins, remains an authoritative but brilliantly different story of the city.

Tom Watkins wrote about his co-author: "Like Rafael Sabatini's Scaramouche, Roger was born with the gift of laughter and sense that the world was mad. Roger never lost his gift of laughter, but unlike Scaramouche, who merely tried to survive in his world, Roger spent most of his adult life trying to improve his. He had the wit of a cynic but the hope of a romantic, and with an obsidian intelligence that cut through fat to the bone of things, he struggled to make people understand how to get things right. The man never had a bad idea — only impossible ones that frequently were made possible. He made the difference."

Scow Schooners of San Francisco Bay, as edited by his wife Nancy and published by the California History Center at De Anza College, includes many historic photographs acquired by the National Maritime Museum at San Francisco long after Roger's thesis was finished. Additional interviews made by Roger Olmsted and myself have been included.

A generous grant from the National Maritime Museum Association and individual donations made it possible to bring this lively work out of the stacks of research libraries and put it into the hands of those who love vessels that sail, pictures of them, and stories about them from the men who were there.

Karl Kortum, Chief Curator
National Maritime Museum
February 1987

National Maritime Museum,
San Francisco

A Catalogue of Bay Shipping . . . Millen Griffith's famous tug Monarch *ploughs through an unusual group. The Italian fisherman lifts his sail to watch her pass, and a scow schooner waits for the wind. A sailing man-of-war, a walking-beam ferry and a Cape Horn grain ship are farther down San Francisco Bay.*

Introduction

Among the more lovable and eccentric of San Francisco's contributions to the history of technology was the scow schooner. Like steam beer and the cable car, the scow was a minor civic institution. It was also one of the more unusual types of local sailing craft developed in the United States during the nineteenth century. These unlikely craft did not suit preconceptions of what a boat should look like. The idea expressed in the design, as in the case of the cable car, seemed too simple to work.

Yet the scow schooner was a thoroughly effective and practical vessel for the transport of bulk cargoes on San Francisco Bay and its tributaries. A fifty or sixty ton scow could lift as much as a hundred tons of hay, brick, grain, sand, or lumber — to mention some of the more common goods that they carried. Their broad and unobstructed decks and great stability allowed stowage of most of their load topside, facilitating loading and unloading, while their flat bottoms allowed them to lie conveniently on the mud at low tide in tiny estuaries among their ports of call. Scows were cheap to build and to operate. While these qualities are obvious enough, one would expect a craft of such description to go about at the end of a towline. But the scows went about by themselves, and the sight of a square sailboat beating smartly to windward, its helmsman standing on an upper rung of a long ladder in order to see over the haystack on deck, seemed almost as strange a hundred years ago as it would today.

It is not unfitting that the clipper-ship should popularly represent "the days of sail" in America, for the Yankee Clippers were among the finest and best-handled sailing vessels that ever put to sea. Yet the era of the clipper was a short interlude in the development of sailing vessels, even in the development of sailing vessels in America in the nineteenth century. The San Francisco run, which had been one of the most important stimuli to the construction of fast sailing ships, lost its urgency with the decline of the gold rush and the improvement of the Panama route. The clippers were replaced by "down-easters," a type that never seemed to catch the popular imagination but which many naval architects and historians have considered superior to clippers. And the clippers were preceded by the fine packet-ships which gave the United States its short-lived supremacy in North Atlantic passenger traffic.

If down-easters and packets are often overlooked, it is not surprising that most of the smaller sailing craft of the nineteenth century, such as the scow schooner, have been almost forgotten. But these craft were more important to the American economy than their larger sisters. It would have been inconceivable that the United States' tremendous coastal and inland traffic should have ceased or been carried in foreign vessels, as was an increasingly large share of the nation's foreign trade as the nineteenth century passed. Not only were the smaller sailing vessels important to the economy of the United States, but the multitude of different types developed for different purposes were interesting in themselves.[1]

The commerce of San Francisco encouraged the East Coast construction of clippers during the gold rush period and down-easters during the grain boom of the 1870s and 1880s, and also produced its share of locally constructed smaller sailing craft. The hundreds of miles of navigable rivers, creeks and sloughs connecting San Francisco with the Central Valley and the hinterland surrounding the bays of San Francisco required the extensive use of water transportation. In addition to this inland navigation, an enormous coastwise trade, particularly in lumber from the Pacific northwest, demanded a large fleet of sailing vessels.

As in other parts of the United States, the boat-builders of San Francisco and the California coast developed different types of vessels to suit the conditions of various uses. First two-masted, then three- and four-masted schooners were built for the coastwise lumber trade, while smaller vessels of the same general type were employed in lighter coast-wise traffic and on San Francisco Bay. The Italian fishermen of San Francisco developed a lateen-rigged craft of Mediterranean design which was unique among American sailing craft; the Chinese "shrimpers" employed San Francisco-built junks. The Whitehall boat, familiar in New York Harbor, appeared on San Francisco Bay as the "water-taxi" for merchants, boarding-house runners, ship-chandlers and others whose business took them out to the ships. Shallow-draft sloops called "plungers" operated in the oyster commerce and other light trades and were often used as pleasure-craft; the early yachts on the bay often bore a strong resemblance to plungers.

The origin of the San Francisco scows is obscure. Howard Chapelle found that sailing scows were used in New England in late colonial times and that the type appeared in many forms and in many places during the nineteenth century. Yet the San Francisco scow seems to have been a purely local

development, possibly growing out of crude and hastily built craft of gold rush days. Sloops and schooners identified as "scows" in custom house records were built at San Francisco in 1850; as early as 1848 a builder at Santa Cruz suggestively christened one of his products *Bloody Box*. A close to definitive search of photographs and prints of gold rush years has failed to identify any craft that looks much like a scow schooner — but it is clear that by 1860 the type was popular and well developed.

Sometimes called the square-toed packet of San Francisco Bay, the vessel was a two-masted, flat-bottomed, centerboard schooner with a transom — that is, square — bow and stem. Hundreds of scows were built between the gold rush and the 1906 earthquake. They operated all over San Francisco Bay and its tributaries, carrying hay, grain, brick, coal, lumber, salt, sand and nearly every other conceivable type of bulk cargo. Appearing with the need for a cheap, shallow-draft sailing craft capable of carrying a fairly large load, scow schooners disappeared with the spread of large motor-trucks and good roads.

It is the purpose of this book to describe, in some detail, the development and use of these vessels: the sort of cargoes that scows carried and where they took them; the sort of men who sailed the scows and the life that they led; the way in which the scows were operated and the nature of the vessels. Emphasis has been placed on what is probably best described as "life in the scows" and on the scow as a type of sailing craft — its design, construction and capabilities.

Chapter I

Entrance to San Francisco

Entrance to the Sacramento River

Courtesy of Bancroft Library

Engravings from Commander Cadawaller Ringgold's 1851 Charts of San Francisco Bay and the Sacramento River

His description follows . . .

"During the years 1849 and 1850 when the tide of emigration was beyond all example, and when the magnificent expanse of waters groaned under the weight of commerce, the anchorage of San Francisco was crowded with richly laden ships, all eager to transport their valuable cargoes to the mining region through the unexplored mazes of extensive bays and rivers and while thousands of human beings were anxiously flocking thither, often in open boats, ill suited to the exposed navigation leading to the interior.

West Fork   Middle Fork

Mark for entering the second section of the Middle Fork of the Sacramento River

West Fork   Middle Fork   Sacramento River

Marks for entering the Sacramento and its Forks at their confluence

. . . The enterprising citizens of San Francisco . . . in absence of any authentic charts saw the necessity of careful and immediate surveys . . . Being at that time in California, I was required to undertake the laborious and toilsome duty of surveying a vast and unknown sea, buoying out the channels and removing the many obstacles attending intercourse with the mines . . . The survey and charts are the results of my own experience, and have cost me much labor. I desire they may be fairly and fully tested, by intelligent, practical navigators, for whose security and advantage they were originally designed, in absence of more elaborate and scientific productions."

Cadawaller Ringgold, Commander, U.S. Navy

The Great Inland Sea —
Early San Francisco Bay Navigation

The bays of San Francisco constitute an almost completely landlocked body of water nearly 65 miles long and covering an area of some 450 square miles. There are two entrances to this inland sea: the Golden Gate, through which the waters of the Pacific flood and ebb, and the Straits of Carquinez, through which the drainage of the great Central Valley of California pours. Beyond the straits open the wide reaches of Suisun Bay and the lower channels of the Sacramento and San Joaquin rivers, where the surrounding lands are very flat and little above the level of the sea, and the rivers are divided into many channels with many inter-connecting sloughs. A map will show better than any other means of description that the entire bay and river system is an obstacle to any means of land transportation, but a natural highway for water traffic. The difficulties faced by the land travelers in traversing the bay and delta regions were discovered by the earliest Spanish explorers of the area. In 1772, Don Pedro Fages was forced to abandon his attempt to reach Point Reyes by land when he reached the shores of Carquinez Straits; Juan Bautista de Anza, in 1776, explored to the east along the south shore of the straits and Suisun Bay but finally found it impossible to proceed further to either the north or east without boats.[2]

The Indians who lived around the shores of the bay at this time used a canoe-shaped boat made out of long tules. A drawing made by Louis Choris, artist for the Russian exploration expedition which visited San Francisco Bay in 1816, shows two Indian men, with a woman, paddling one of these craft across the bay. The paddlers used double-ended paddles with long, narrow blades shaped like an arrow-head.

These boats were unsinkable, as each tule was a separate float, but the bottom did not remain water-tight.[3] The Spanish had little use for these Indian *balsas*, yet it seems to have been some time before they constructed boats of their own.

The Mission of San Francisco de Asis was founded in 1776 and the Mission of Santa Clara and the pueblo of San Jose the next year. Twenty years later the mission of San Jose was founded. During these twenty years, and the next twenty, there was little or no trade between the San Francisco settlements and the outside world; the presidio of San Francisco was no more than a feeble outpost against Russian expansion. Since all the settlements were on the west and south sides of San Francisco Bay, communications between them seem to have been carried on by land. It is doubtful that the Spaniards used any boats on the bay, other than those belonging to the supply ships that occasionally came from Mexico.

In 1815, when Commandant Arguello began repairs on the disintegrating San Francisco presidio, he was forced to send men to cut timber completely around the south end of the bay, up the east shore, and around the northern side of San Pablo Bay, in order to reach Corte Madera, in present Marin County. The men crossed Carquinez Straits on the tule rafts of the Indians. In Corte Madera, an English carpenter helped them build a suitable boat to carry the timber through Raccoon Straits and across the Golden Gate to the presidio. When Governor Bola heard of the expedition, he reproved Arguello for building a boat without his permission.[4] Certainly, if the Spaniards had possessed any craft capable of carrying a moderate load, Arguello would not have put himself and his

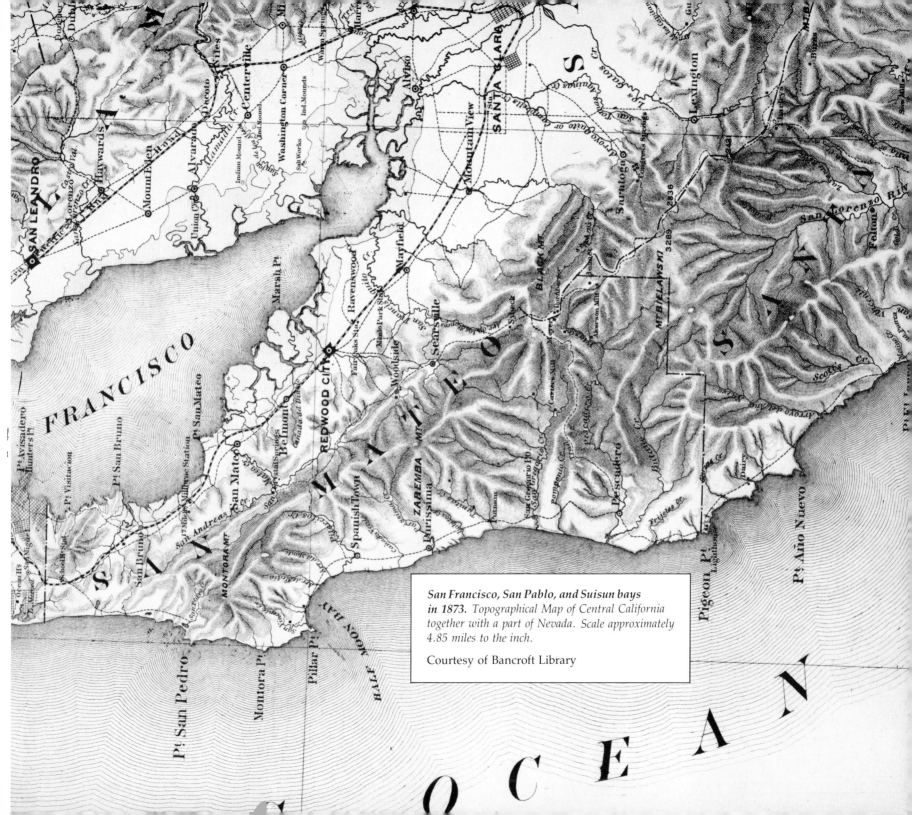

San Francisco, San Pablo, and Suisun bays in 1873. Topographical Map of Central California together with a part of Nevada. Scale approximately 4.85 miles to the inch.

Courtesy of Bancroft Library

men to so much trouble.

The mission of San Rafael was founded in December 1819, and that of San Francisco de Solano in 1823, and communication with the settlements to the south must have required the building or procurement of small boats. Furthermore, the formal opening of California to foreign trade, in 1821, demanded the use of suitable craft to collect hides and tallow and bring them to the ships. Since the founding of the missions, the cattle herds had grown larger and larger, as there was no market for the hides and tallow. It is estimated that in 1822 the Mission San Francisco de Asis, or Dolores, owned 160,000 head of cattle, sheep, and horses, besides harvesting an annual crop of 60,000 bushels of grain.[5] The missions of Santa Clara and San Jose also had tremendous herds. John Begg and Company, an English firm, entered into a contract with the missions in 1821 to take all the hides they had to offer as well as 25,000 arrobas[6] of tallow each year. The following year brought the Boston brig Sachem to California in quest of hides and tallow, and in each succeeding year, San Francisco Bay became more important as a highway of commerce.

About 1824, William Richardson, who had deserted from an English whaler two years before in San Francisco Harbor, constructed a small boat named Maria Antonis, and shortly thereafter he operated two small schooners. In these vessels he transported hides, tallow, and wheat from the missions to foreign trading ships. He charged twelve cents per hide, twenty-five cents for a 500-pound bag of tallow, and twenty-five cents for two and one-half bushels of wheat.[7]

It seems that the mission Indians also built some small, schooner-rigged craft for transporting hides and tallow. "Under the instructions and guidance of the priests and after plans drawn by them, the Indians at the missions around the bay built schooners or launches in which the missions sent down their produce to the vessels in Yerba Buena Cove and brought back the goods received in exchange."[8] William Heath Davis also mentioned "shipwright" among the trades learned by the Indians from the Padres.[9] Richard Henry Dana described the hide boats of the missions as "launches, manned by Indians, and capable of carrying from five to six hundred hides apiece . . . ."[10] He depicted the boat in which he went to gather wood for his ship as a "large, schooner-rigged, open launch, which we had hired of the mission . . . ."[11]

The origin of all these boats is rather hazy. After Richardson started operating his boats, the missions of San Jose and Dolores "procured two 30-ton schooners built at Fort Ross."[12] Yet there is some question whether Richardson raised his boats from the bay, operated them for the missions, or bought them from the missions, if they were the mission boats of which Dana wrote.[13] In any event, it seems probable that two or three launches of about thirty tons were adequate for San Francisco Bay traffic between 1825 and 1835.

Ranchos, great and small, developed around San Francisco Bay during the 1830s and 1840s, while the secularized missions disappeared. Although none of the herds were so large as that of the Mission Dolores in 1822, and despite the large annual slaughter for the visiting hide-ships, the area boasted 200,000 cattle in 1838.[14]

By the late 1830s, the village of Yerba Buena was an established commercial community. Credits for hides and tallow were the banknotes of the day and were used in exchange for merchandise. Nathan Spear of Yerba Buena, employed two small schooners, Isabel and Nicholas, to carry his goods to ranchos around the bay.[15] When Johann Sutter arrived in California in 1839, he chartered these two schooners to take his company and equipment up the Sacramento River. He also used a four-oared boat which he had brought with him to California.[16] The launch and an occasional trip by Nicholas or Isabel constituted the river traffic until, with the purchase of Russian possessions at Bodega and Fort Ross in 1841, Sutter acquired a schooner.

The Sacramento, as Sutter called her, initiated what might be called the first regular packet service on the river. She has

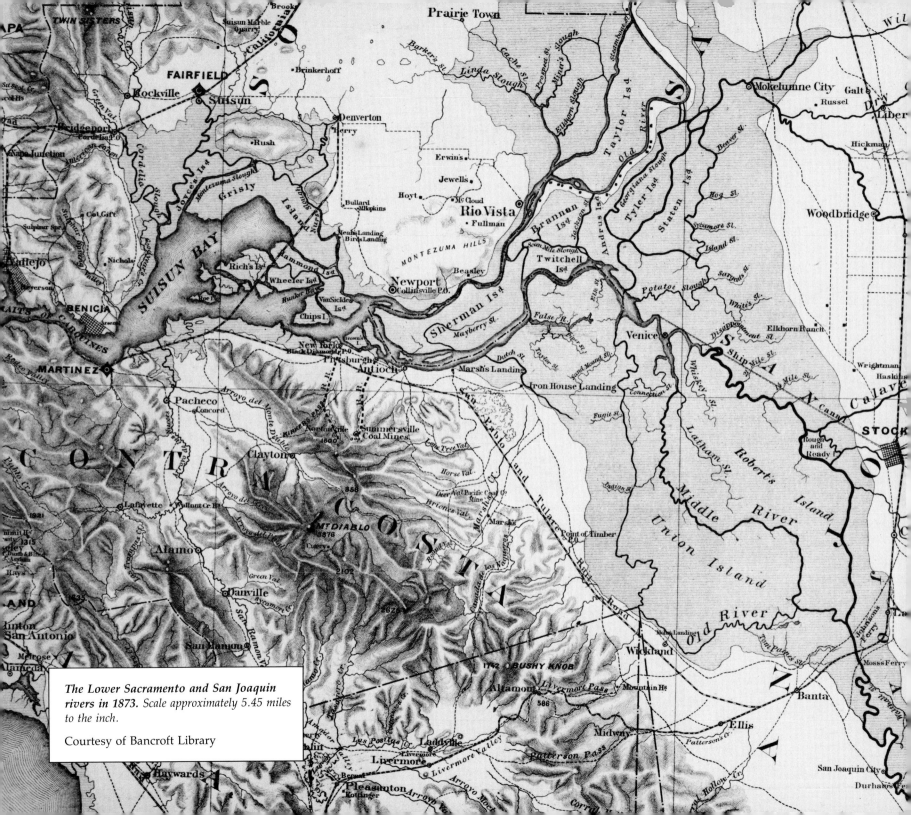

*The Lower Sacramento and San Joaquin
rivers in 1873.* Scale approximately 5.45 miles
to the inch.

Courtesy of Bancroft Library

been variously described as a vessel of 17, 22, and 40 tons.[17] George McKintry, one of the pioneers at Sutter's Fort, writing to his friend Edward Kem in 1851, spoke of "The lovely Sacramento, which in our time was only disturbed by the well-known, fast-sailing, copper and copper-fastened clipper-schooner, *Sacramento*, Youckmomney, master . . .!"[18] The description is obviously a play on the packet advertisements prominent in the *Alta California* in 1850 and 1851, so the *Sacramento* was no doubt a none too desirable vessel.

Quite a number of craft seem to have been working on the bay and rivers by 1844, besides the vessels already mentioned. These included the lighters *Yuba, San Francisquito, Rosalia, Joselita, Guadalupe,* and *Lundresa*.[19] *Lundresa* was built by John C. Davis in Napa Creek and is said to have been used by Sutter to carry grain down to the Russian ships in San Francisco.[20] *Guadalupe*, nine tons, was used by Richardson; and *Joselita*, three tons, by Victor Castro. Possibly Davis, a shipwright by trade, built some of these lighters, other than *Lundresa*, and some of them may have been much earlier, possibly the mission boats referred to by Dana. It is likely that they carried some sort of rig — it certainly would have been a long pull from Yerba Buena to Sutter's Fort. Another boat built by Davis in Napa Creek was the schooner *Susana*, launched in 1841; *Susana* was used "outside," running to Monterey, Mazatlan, and other points.[21]

Trade increased with the foreign — particularly American — population of California, and it changed rapidly after the American occupation of Yerba Buena, or San Francisco, as it soon was called. A thousand people had settled in San Francisco by 1848, and two hundred buildings had been erected. Boats for the bay and coasting trades were being built nearby. The 67-ton schooner *Lola* was built in Santa Cruz in 1846[22], and in 1848 at least four small sloops and schooners were constructed there — the *Charles and Edward, Mary, Bonnie Jean,* and *Bloody Box*.[23] Probably these boats were built in Santa Cruz because of the proximity of timber. *Mary's* coasting

license shows that she was built for three gentlemen of Corte Madera, and *Bonnie Jean* was so small that she almost always was employed in the bay trade. Most of the timber used in San Francisco was obtained, at this time, from Santa Cruz and Bodega. In April of 1847, W. A. Leidesdorff, one of the leading merchants of San Francisco, notified the public that he was "prepared to fill orders for all kinds of lumber, at Bodega, or at this place, as low as it can be afforded in the country . . ."[24] The first steam sawmill in California had been erected at Bodega in 1843.[25]

The news of gold at Sutter's mill all but emptied San Francisco in the summer of 1848, but as the inhabitants started drifting back to town and thousands of Argonauts poured in from the East, some people decided that it was more profitable to carry gold hunters and their freight up and down the rivers than to dig in the hills.

Sam Brannan, one of San Francisco's most successful entrepreneurs and the city's first millionaire, had the foresight to buy the *Gusonita* for $10,000 from Jean Vioget. A ship's longboat that had been decked over and schooner rigged, *Gusonita* took advantage of the overwhelming press of river traffic bound for the mines. William Robinson Grimshaw was employed as a combination skipper and bookkeeper. In one year's time this decked-over sailing launch cleared a profit of $50,000 "in gold in buckskin sacks; these were nailed up in a strong wooden box and put on the launch." Grimshaw's description of making his way up the delta is an eloquent account: "In passing through narrow Steamboat Slough (then called Merritt's) the branches of the large sycamore trees growing at the river's edge meet and form an almost continous arch overhead. From the slough up, the trunks and branches of the trees protruded from the bank far out into the river on each side . . . how difficult was navigation for a small craft drifting with the raging currents of the spring freshlets . . . . At night the tules west of the Sacramento would sometimes be burning and the elk and deer running affrighted before the

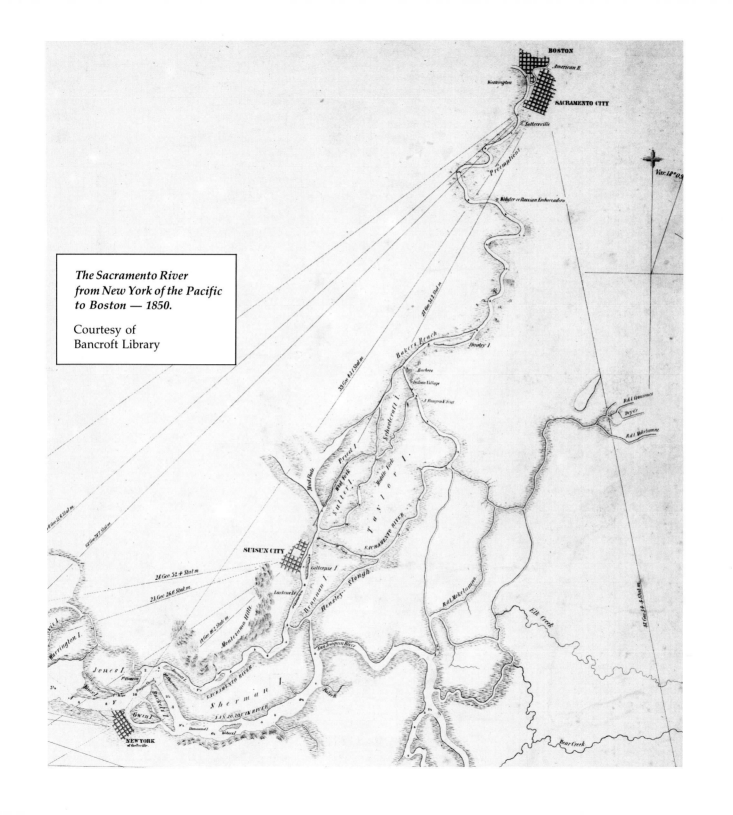

The Sacramento River from New York of the Pacific to Boston — 1850.

Courtesy of Bancroft Library

fire would make a rumbling like distant thunder.

"No description can do justice of a nighttime passed in the warm months. Clouds of mosquitos rendered sleep utterly out of the question. No matter how hard a man worked all day at the oar or otherwise, the only way of getting through the night was to build a fire that would make as much smoke as possible, and walk about until morning, flapping a handkerchief before the face . . . . The great gold rush of California had set in. Every imaginable kind of craft from a whaleboat to the barque *Whitton* of 500 tons came up the river carrying passengers with their baggage. Boats were rowed all the way from San Francisco. Many of these . . . would enter some one of the network of sloughs and row about for days before they were extracted from the labyrinth."[26]

Spring of 1849 saw the beginning of an estimated 87,000 immigrants arrive in California, a very large number of these heading upriver for the mines. Yet shipping was very scarce that spring, and lumber freights from Santa Cruz ran forty dollars per thousand feet.[27] Despite costs, boatbuilders and merchants were quick to rise to the need, and during 1849, 1850, and 1851 scores of coasting and bay craft were built. Boats were built at Santa Cruz, Monterey, Bodega, Marysville, Sacramento, Stockton, Napa Creek, San Rafael, Angel Island, and Rancho de Las Pulgas, but by far the greatest number were built in San Francisco.[28]

Trade up and down the rivers was more than brisk. On February 1, 1849, the *Alta California*, discussing the recent history of San Francisco, said: "The cost of transportation and the means thereof, had gradually risen, until the wages of boatmen, instead of . . . from ten to forty dollars per month, were . . . up to one hundred dollars, and the value of launches [sic] which originally cost from one hundred to two thousand, now ranged from five hundred to ten thousand. Freight from San Francisco to Sutter's Embarcadero, a distance of some one hundred and sixty miles, was three dollars per one hundred pounds, and the passage money for each passenger was ten dollars." There were no steamers on the river at this time; the schooner *Emily and Jane* advertised "accommodations of 200 deck passengers;"[29] and by August, there were at least forty-two vessels sailing more or less regularly between San Francisco and the river ports.[30]

In 1850, steamer competition cut freight rates in half, and sailing packet advertisements disappeared from the *Alta California*. The price of small sailing vessels dropped considerably but remained rather high. Sale prices of thirteen vessels of from twenty to fifty tons sold in 1851, 1852, and 1853, suggests that prices had stabilized themselves fairly well, a schooner of from thirty to forty tons costing between $2000 and $5000 depending on the age and condition of the boat.[31]

Most of the boats engaged in the river trade seem to have been sloops and schooners, sharp-bowed and round-bottomed, and many of them must have been very roughly built. Many even more elementary boats appeared, too — vessels of the scow type. Probably most of these scows bore little resemblance to the later San Francisco scow schooners, but they were the precursors of the type that was to become exceedingly popular on San Francisco Bay.

Chapter II

National Maritime Museum,
San Francisco

On a misty morning in Mission Bay *... A pair of scows wait for a breeze
... a pair of barges wait for a tow ... down-easters wait for cargos and
grain from California's San Joaquin and Sacramento valleys — wheat that
produced the world famous "California white velvet flour" and brought an
immense foreign fleet here in the 1880s.*

The Scow Sloop Came First . . . *The 1850s saw a large number of sloop rigged scows built in San Francisco, as this* <u>Alta California</u> *ad suggests: "MARKET BOAT – For Sale – One SCOW SLOOP, with centreboard [sic], 42 feet long, 15 feet wide, 4 feet 4 inches deep, with mast, gaffs, booms, bowsprit, windlass, shrouds and jibstays, anchors, chain cables, sweeps, oars, sails and rigging, and one yawl for do, all complete. Macondray & Co.," December, 1850.*

In later years, with the building of larger scows, the handier schooner rig became more popular. Note the flat sheer and generally box-like appearance of this early San Francisco scow.

National Maritime Museum,
San Francisco

San Francisco's Own Square-Toed Packets

Dozens of local types of commercial sailing craft evolved in the United States during the nineteenth century. For the most part, this variety represented attempts of local boat owners and builders to produce craft suited to particular working conditions. Development of these many kinds of watercraft was influenced by local geographic and economic conditions, by availability of building materials and skilled builders, and by tradition and fashion. While each local type developed the way it did for good reason, it was not necessarily the only kind of craft that might have served the purpose.

Were it possible to combine the ultimate in speed, seaworthiness, strength, handiness, shoal draft, cargo capacity, low building, maintenance, and operating cost in one boat, only one kind of sailing vessel would have evolved. But every type of craft developed had to be a compromise between some or all of these qualities, and the first basis for this compromise lay in the conditions to which the vessel was to be subjected. For example, the extreme clipper ship sacrificed cargo capacity to speed, while the New Bedford whaler did just the opposite.

As has been pointed out, shipping on San Francisco Bay and its tributaries in 1849 became so profitable that any sailing craft capable of running between river ports and the bay would have become an economic success. Steamboat competition, however, soon took away from the schooners the most lucrative trades — the passenger and fast freight businesses. Sailing workboats held their own in the bulk carrying trades, but as business conditions became more settled profit margins declined. The time was ripe for the development of a type of sailing vessel *suited* to the transportation of bulk cargo on San Francisco Bay and upriver and not merely *used* for this purpose.

Navigation of these inland waterways did not demand a craft of exceptional seaworthiness nor did bulk carrying trades require high speed. The possibility of compromising these two qualities without adversely affecting the utility of the boat permitted development of a scow-type vessel — a cheap, strong, and burdensome craft that did the most work at the least cost. Because of these desirable qualities, the scow soon became popular on San Francisco Bay.

The scow schooners of San Francisco were handy sailing craft. When a seaman described a vessel as "handy," he meant that she possessed a combination of desirable qualities: she was easy to work, handled well under different conditions of wind and water, tacked to windward smartly, and maneuvered well in close quarters. Handiness implied respectable performance, but not necessarily speed. The scow type of hull is capable of development into a craft of great speed, but the San Francisco scow schooners were much too heavily built and the upward curve of their run (the after part of the bottom) was too abrupt and steep for them to be driven faster than a conventional hull of the same size.

It was this kind of handiness that attracted Captain John Leale's eye when he first went to work on the Sacramento River in 1865. He found that "slow freight from San Francisco was shipped by schooners — at first sharp-bow vessels, later vessels of the scow type, which is square bow and stern and flat bottomed. These latter would carry more cargo on lighter draft, besides working better in close quarters."[1]

An example of the sort of scow schooner being built in San

Francisco in 1865 was *War Eagle*. Henry Hall, taking notes for a report on shipbuilding in the United States for the Tenth Census, measured and sketched her.[2]

Henry Hall notes:

length on deck	*58' 3"*	*fore boom*	*28'*
beam	*20'*	*fore gaff*	*18'*
depth of hold	*5 or 6'*	*main boom*	*38'*
bowsprit	*18'*	*main gaff*	*20'*
jibboom	*32'*	*register tonnage*	*38 tons*
masts	*75'*	*cargo capacity*	*70 tons*
topmast	*28'*		

Here was the San Francisco Bay scow schooner in substantially its final form, although differences between individual scows at any given time might be greater than any differences between the *War Eagle* and the average scow of later years.

While it is certain that the scow schooner was widely employed on San Francisco Bay by 1865, the origin of the type is obscure. During the early days of the gold rush, many of the vessels arriving in San Francisco carried knocked-down lighters on board to be used in unloading the ship, as San Francisco then possessed no port facilities. Some of these vessels almost certainly were rigged and used as common carriers during the gold rush period when shallow-draft shipping was scarce.

Sailing scows were built in San Francisco as early as 1850; at least two schooner-rigged scows, *New England* and *Niantic*,

and one sloop-rigged scow, *J. A. Sutter*, were built that year.[3] Many other vessels described simply as "scows" were also constructed at about the same time[4], but it is not known if they carried a rig. Nor is there evidence that *New England*, *Niantic*, or any other of these vessels bore any close resemblance to later scow schooners.

The scow type is by nature very easy to build, and may be subject to considerable variation in design and construction, depending upon the abilities, inclinations, and prejudices of the builders. Since people flocked to California from all over America and from many other parts of the world during the gold rush, and both amateurs and professionals among them took to building boats, the early San Francisco Bay scows may have been of several different types imported from anywhere that sailing scows were used, which was just about everywhere.

As Howard Chapelle observed, "The most primitive of the flat-bottomed hull-form, the scow, was employed in great numbers and had an extraordinary spread throughout North America. Not only were there examples of the type in use along the entire Atlantic Coast, from the Maritime Provinces to Mexico, but also on the Great Lakes, on Champlain, and on any of the rivers large enough to be used for small-craft navigation. Flat-bottomed boats and vessels of scow construction were used on the Pacific Coast and in the Canadian northwest as well. Often the scow was of elementary form, rectangular on deck, and rough, simple, and undistinguishable in character and appearance."[5]

The San Francisco scow could have been a descendant of one or more of the other scow types in use at the time, or it may have evolved from rigged barges and lighters. The San Francisco scow schooner apparently *did* undergo local development, and was not borrowed whole from some other locality, for not only was the type quite unlike the scows used in other parts of America, but scow men do not generally agree as to its origin.

The San Francisco Scow at Her Best... Lew Young *shows all the elements of grace inherent in good design, whether it be scow design or yacht design. A graceful sheet, smartly raking ends, and handsome rig are assets to any craft.*

National Maritime Museum, San Francisco

There is some evidence that the hull form of the earlier scows was cruder than that of later vessels. A Danish sailor who landed in San Francisco in 1859 described the scow type as being "built almost square, something like a Danish mud scow."[6] The hulk of *Young America*, built in 1859, was visible until the early 1950s on the banks of the Alameda estuary. She appears to have been somewhat barge-like, having relatively straight sides and a flat sheer.[7] The *Garibaldi*, built in 1861, is seen racing alongside the much later *Granger*; the photograph on page 37 shows that *Garibaldi* had less sheer and a generally less attractive hull form than her rival. Two still earlier scows, *Redwood* (1852) and *Nimrod* (1853), have been cited by one builder as examples of "square-built" scows. However, not enough pictures and accurate descriptions of scows built prior to 1860 have turned up to warrant any definite conclusion as to the type's development.

Whatever its origin, the scow type became very popular on San Francisco Bay during the 1860s and 1870s. Henry Hall briefly summarizes the characteristics of San Francisco scows and their activities as he saw them in 1881: "A large number of scow schooners are employed in the bay and on the Sacramento River and its tributaries, in freighting brick, hay, grain bags, and produce. At the brick wharf in San Francisco nearly 30 of these little schooners can be seen almost every day, unloading. They are from 40 to 50 feet long, two masters, carrying three men to work them. Their load is generally carried on deck. They are handy and pretty smart."[8] The fact that as many as thirty scows might be seen unloading brick gives some indication of how numerous they were; at least two hundred or more scows must have been in operation at the time, for certainly not all of the brick scows would have been unloading at the wharf at once, and the brick trade was only one of many trades.

17

National Maritime Museum, San Francisco

Lazy Afternoon on the Sacramento . . . *The* Wonder *rides light with no breeze stirring. Behind her, a rare bald-headed scow shares the shimmering heat and come sundown — the mosquitoes.*

Some of the qualities which popularized the scow have been mentioned or implied; the square-toed packet cost less to build than the conventional schooner of equivalent cargo capacity; it carried a large load on a comparatively short overall length and had the advantage of carrying its cargo almost entirely on deck, greatly facilitating loading and unloading; its shallow draft, even when loaded, gave the boat a wider range of navigation than more conventional types; its simple sail plan could be handled easily by two men — even one, if necessary — and the craft's large centerboard and rudder made it relatively quick-turning. While the scow was hardly an ideal vessel for ocean crossings, it was quite capable, if reasonably handled, of meeting San Francisco Bay at its worst. Scows often ventured beyond the Golden Gate to Drake's Bay, Bolinas, Point Reyes and Paper Mill Creek, and some are known to have sailed to Alaska during the Klondike rush.[9]

Speed was not a primary consideration in designing San Francisco scows, but not all of them were slow. Speaking of scows in general, Howard Chapelle observes, "The sailing scows were often quite remarkable for their surprising weatherliness and turn of speed under sail. . . . Many of them, due to their beam and flat bottom, were very powerful craft that could carry a large spread of sail in proportion to their displacement. Some had long, sweeping lines in sides and bottom that also produced speed and steadiness on the helm as well. The large sloop- and schooner-rigged scows were often smart sailers when light, and there are numerous instances recorded when these big scows showed their sterns to fast commercial sailing craft and yachts."[10]

Indeed, many San Francisco yachtsmen did see only the stern of a scow when it was sailing light and off the wind, for under the proper conditions, the San Francisco scow schooner could make very fast runs. The *Fourth of July*, with a crew anxious to make home port on Christmas eve, was reported to have run from Stockton to Petaluma in seven hours, which would imply an average speed of over ten knots — probably eight for the boat and two or three for the tide.[11] *Fourth of July* was built in 1861 and measured sixty feet on deck, with a beam of twenty-two feet, and yet, she had no great reputation as a fast sailer.

Scows differed very greatly in their sailing abilities, since speed was easily compromised by poor design. Better builders constructed scows that had all of the virtues of the type and were fairly fast as well, but many of the scows, particularly in the early days, seem just to have sprung out of the shores of the bay. Henry Hall found that "There are few regular yards, the work being done by carpenters, who are hired to do the job, or by amateurs."[12] Vessels were constructed in this casual fashion not only in San Francisco, but at many points around the shores of the bay — at Vallejo, Benicia, Corte Madera, Oakland, Alameda, Mt. Eden, San Rafael, Gallinas Creek, South San Francisco, Redwood City, and even on Yerba Buena Island.[13] Apparently many scows were put together on the properties of farmers and ranchers who needed boats to carry their goods to market or to bring in supplies. For example, the scow sloop *Pride of Wood Island* was built by the Lorentzen family in 1887 on Wood Island, a small tract (long since dredged away in the interests of flood control) in the middle of the Sacramento River, opposite the town of Rio Vista. The Lorentzens used the boat for some years to transport persons, property, and produce to and from the island.[14] It is impossible to estimate how many scows were built by amateurs and by carpenters hired for the single job, as there is little or no official record of these vessels, and they may have disappeared at an early date because of inferior construction.

At the other end of the scale, several notable San Francisco Bay ship builders also tried their hand at constructing scows. Patrick Henry Tiernan, one of the most famous of the early shipbuilders, built *Elko* and *Truckee* to carry freight for the Central Pacific before freight steamers appeared on the bay,[15] and Matthew Turner, San Francisco's most notable builder of wooden ships, launched many scows from his Benicia yard.[16]

Proud Launching Day at Anderson's Yard . . .
With flags flying, Undine is launched in
1902: a handsome sight, she is 78 feet long,
27 feet across, 6.3 feet in depth and 95 tons.
Her cabin is under a raised poop and divided
into several small cabins, unusual in their
exceptionally handsome fittings.

The Builders and Their Tools . . .
Anderson's crew with broadaxe,
caulking hammer, topmaul, saw and
plane. The Alpine is on the ways for
repair. Fourth from the right, the
bearded fellow holding a plane is Neil
McAdams, a legendary artist with the
broadaxe and adze. According to H. C.
Thomsen, the former owner of a nearby
yard, "once McAdam had gotten out
[shaped] a piece of timber with axe or
adze he did not need to use the plane very
much."

The Birth of a Scow . . . "Pop" Anderson's gang pose aboard a nearly completed scow, Charles W.. Charlie Waack, the owner is the large man standing in the center. Caulking mallets are much in evidence, and launching day is not far off. The youngest apprentice in the crowd would be the one who periodically trotted across Innes Avenue to fill a large pail with Albion's brew. As first year apprentice he only got 50 cents a day but he could look forward after four years to getting $4 a day on repair work (which was dirtier and sometimes dangerous).

"Pop" Anderson (below) was one of the many North Germans and Scandinavians who worked as caulkers and carpenters, joiners and riggers in the dozen yards that persisted on San Francisco's Hunters Point until the 1930s, but in Anderson's case he came to own the yard.

All views, National Maritime Museum, San Francisco

But the center of scow building activity during most of the years when sailing vessels were important in bay trade was Hunters Point, where August and Willie Schultze, Nichols and Weaver, Thomsen, Seimer, Dirks, Erickson, Ervin, Goebel, Stone, O. F. L. Farenkamp, "Pop" Anderson, and William Munder had their yards during the 1880s, 1890s, and the early years of this century.[17] Scores of scow schooners were launched from these yards, and every spring many more were hauled up on the ways there for scraping, painting, and other maintenance.

These boatyards shared the southern waterfront with San Francisco's Butchertown, after a city ordinance in 1869 moved the slaughterhouses from Ninth and Brannan on Mission Creek to the more isolated Islais Creek drainage. From Fairfax to Custer, on both sides of Railroad Avenue (Third Street), tanneries, slaughterhouses, sheep pens, cattle corrals, packing houses, tripe works, tallow works, glue factories and fertilizer companies spread over the former salt marsh, with wharves to dump waste extending over the bay water. Four blocks southeast of Railroad Avenue, Hunters Point Road curved around the southern waterfront where many clusters of marine ways on the shallow shoreline beaches appear on maps from 1882 up through 1929. These boatyards shared the water's edge with even more informal Chinese shrimp fishermen who put up clusters of tiny dwellings, dried their shrimp, mended their nets, and launched their junks alongside the scows.[18]

Of the several Hunters Point yard owners, William Munder and his sons were the most prolific scow builders. William Munder came to California in 1865 as carpenter in a German ship.[19] The ship's captain apparently thought so highly of his crew that he anchored in the middle of the bay, and Munder had to swim more than a mile to escape to the Alameda shore. Wishing to keep out of sight until the ship left, he walked until he came to Mt. Eden, where he was hired by a carpenter who was building a scow schooner. The next year he went to

North Beach, where he built the scow *Lorenz and William;* then he moved to Butchertown. The yards were soon driven out by the proximity of the expanding slaughterhouses, and he moved out to Hunters Point. There he prospered, and in 1880 he retired to Petaluma. But within a few months he returned to Hunters Point and bought another yard, which he operated until his death. His sons succeeded him and kept the yard going until 1925.

The Munders, and most of the other scow builders, built scows on the basis of verbal contracts. Very few scows were built from drawings or models — the buyer would tell the builder what size boat he wanted, and the builder would quote a price. The builder then would put the scow together the same way he always built a scow. Various builders had different ideas as to the best hull shape, and these differences were never resolved to the extent that scows became stereotyped.

For example, J. S. Nichols built the 69-foot scow schooner *Nettie* which in 1891, lost by only eight minutes in a three-hour Master Mariner's race to the *Azalene*. Admittedly the *Nettie* was fast for a scow. Her ends were carried out further and were nipped in more sharply than usual. Nichols thought narrow ends, together with placement of the greatest beam abaft of amidships, determined the best form of the scow. He was probably right. On the other hand, William Munder, the most prolific of scow builders, thought that the greatest beam should be well forward and the stern narrower than the bow, basing his theory upon the design of fast-swimming fish. His observation was of dubious utility, but his scows sailed well enough.

The boatyard owners, when they had no contract work and when repair work was slack, would often build a scow on speculation to keep the yard hands busy. If no one bought the vessel immediately, it would be operated on shares with a crew until such time as it could be sold profitably.

The reasonably low cost of scow schooners seems to have remained fairly constant between 1860 and 1910. The

Munder's Boatyard at Hunters Point, A Family Tradition . . .
William Munder started his boatyard in North Beach but moved to Hunters Point, near Pop Anderson's ways. Horses were still used to operate the big capstans that hauled the vessels out of the water for repair. Mrs. William Munder is on the right, in front of the scow schooner.

A Scow Schooner on the Ways . . .
Possibly the scow schooner Erma in the spring of 1904. Her namesake, Erma H. Olsen, was four at the time and did the honors of christening at the launching.

Both views, National Maritime Museum, San Francisco

twenty-two ton *Rock of Cashel*, for example, was worth $1,000 in 1867; in 1876 she sold for the same price.[20] The larger *War Eagle* – thirty-three tons – sold for $2,800 in 1875 and $2,000 a year later. In 1901, Emil Munder built the *Crockett*, a fifty-six ton scow, for $2,150, although this figure was for the hull alone and probably did not include many of the fittings. The ninety-two ton *Matilda* was built in 1905 at a cost of $5,700.[21] As the cost of boats of comparable hull form and construction is in almost direct proportion to their tonnage, it can be seen that the increase in prices during the forty years when the scow was at the peak of its popularity was more the result of an increase in their size than of inflation.

Scows were cheap because labor and materials were cheap. During the thirty years preceding the First World War, the standard boatyard wage at Hunters Point for skilled ship-wrights was around four dollars a day for new construction and five dollars a day for repair work. Repair work paid more because it often required more skill, was dirtier than new work, and sometimes was dangerous. The beginning shipwright looked forward to four years of apprenticeship, and during his first year he was paid but fifty cents a day. Not only was the cost of labor low, as compared to today, but materials also were relatively inexpensive — the best clear Oregon pine cost only twenty dollars per thousand.[22]

That many scows were well built craft and well maintained is proved by the number of years that some of them lasted.

War Eagle, for example, was already sixteen years old when Henry Hall took her measurements in 1881, and she was still running in 1925.[23] *Traveler*, built in 1864, finally succumbed — to termites — in 1940.[24] *Hermine Blum*, *Gas Light*, *Fourth of July*, *Robbie Hunter*, and many others worked the bay and rivers upwards of fifty years. Good materials and good workmanship went into vessels that survived a half-century of hard use.

Typical of the kind of man who built these boats was Neil McAdams, a Nova Scotian who worked in Hunters Point yards for many years. H. C. Thomsen, one of his employers, described his uncommon skill, "We had a short plank to fit in the *Jessie Matson*. It had quite a twist but was too short to steam. I asked Neil if he could hew it out and he took a 12x14 and adzed out a two-and-one-half inch plank. The remarkable thing was that the first time he lifted it up into place, it slipped right in — the twist was just perfect."[25]

There was quite a flurry of scow-building in the first few years of this century, and it generally is estimated that there were about four hundred scows on the bay at this time.[26] But just as the steam engine was driving the square-rigger from the sea, the development of the internal combustion engine threatened the dominion of sail on the inland waterways. Probably the last sailing scow built in San Francisco was the *Edith*, ordered from Emil Munder the day before the great 1906 earthquake.

Chapter III

National Maritime Museum,
San Francisco

***San Francisco Bound* . . .** Covina *beating down Suisun Bay. It was this unlikely sight of a hay stack moving smartly before the wind on open water that caught the public fancy — "hay scow" became the general name for scows regardless of their cargo.*

Annie L . . . *Here Annie L. built in 1900 by Emil Munder, at 67 feet long and measuring about 60 tons, brings in more than 350 bales of hay for San Francisco's horse population. Hayloads were collected from as far away as Sacramento and Milpitas and many informal stopping places along shallow* *sloughs and creeks where the shallow draft vessels could ease off mudbanks at high tides.*

National Maritime Museum, San Francisco

"Hay Scow" on the Bay

Before the day of the internal combustion engine, at least a half-dozen distinct types of sailing craft operated over the hundreds of miles of navigable inland waterways stretching north, south, and east from San Francisco. The scow schooner was probably the most important of these vessels to the area's economic life, and hay was the most characteristic, if not the most important, of the scow's many different cargoes. The nineteenth century moved on hay, much as the twentieth moves on gasoline, and the hay trade was vital to the economy of urban areas, such as San Francisco.

But the San Francisco scow did not acquire the nickname "hay scow" because of an appreciation of its importance to San Francisco's horse population. Rather, the highly unnautical appearance of the scow with a towering deckload of hay impressed itself on the popular imagination to such an extent that "hay scow" seemed the best term to characterize it. Indeed, scows were particularly adapted to the carriage of such bulk cargoes as hay, and some of their fittings and equipment were designed to this end. For example, the wheel was usually mounted on a small platform (called the "pulpit") which could be raised up so that the helmsman could see over a high load.[1]

Quite a number of scows engaged in the hay trade, a business in which they had almost no sailing competition, because the sharp-bowed schooners were not nearly as well suited to carrying such a bulky cargo. The Hay Wharf, on the Third Street Channel, was the focal point of the hay trade, and here a dozen or more scows could often be seen tied two and three abreast and loaded five or six tiers of bales high.[2]

Captain Fred Klebingat remembers the Hay Wharf in 1908: "Leaving Pope and Talbot's lumberyard, we headed out the finger pier that angled out into the channel to accommodate the bay scows or scow schooners unloading hay. The scow schooners were made fast, sometimes three abreast, the inner one busy discharging its cargo. . . . Several bay scows were now discharged and ready for another voyage. They moved to the outer tier, set their lowers, put down the centerboard, let go (some shoving off with the pike pole) and with a rubbing of strakes against their sisters they gathered headway. . . . It took pure seamanship and good judgment to tack in this confined space."[3]

Hay loads were collected from as far afield as Sacramento and Milpitas as well as at many points on shallow creeks and sloughs closed to vessels lacking the scow's shallow draft. Following the introduction of hydraulic mining in the 1850s, the navigation of Suisun Bay and the rivers became increasingly difficult. The San Joaquin, not as deep as the Sacramento to begin with, became so shallow in the 1860s that only light draft vessels could reach Stockton,[4] but a scow loaded with 50 to 75 tons of hay drew only about four feet of water.

Hay was, of course, not the only agricultural product which scows carried down from the hinterland: potatoes, beans, and other vegetables; rye, barley, bran, oats, and, most important of all, wheat, were shipped in large quantities.[5] During the hectic days of the gold rush, central California became a wheat-importing area, and flour sold for as high as $50 a barrel in San Francisco in 1852. High prices and heavy local demand rapidly expanded grain acreage; by the late 1850s some small amounts of wheat were being exported. The first big surplus

Five Tiers to Go . . . Lunch time finds the crew of the Charles W. *in the cabin enjoying the stew that has been simmering on the stove all morning. This is a welcome break from the hard labor of neatly stowing a load of hay. There were five tiers of bales above and two below, over 800 bales of hay, or 80 tons.*

wheat crop was grown in 1860,[6] and in that year over 100 flour mills operated in the state.[7] Most of the wheat was raised in the valleys bordering San Francisco Bay, and steamboats and small sailing craft must have transported all that was sent to San Francisco.

During the 1870s, California became one of the world's great wheat exporting areas. The California wheat shipped, stored, and milled exceptionally well, and commanded high prices in Europe where the appetite for California's "white velvet" flour proved insatiable. California's grain industry not only stimulated the local transportation industry but had a tremendous impact on world shipping. Yards in Maine and England turned out scores of fine square-rigged vessels, primarily for the Cape Horn run to San Francisco.[8] In 1873, 339 vessels carried grain from San Francisco to foreign ports, for which they received $9,173,216 in freight charges — an average of over $27,000 apiece![9] The peak year of the grain

trade came with the great harvest of 1881-82, when 547 sailing ships departed San Francisco with grain.[10]

Suitable facilities for loading grain ships were developed during the 1880s along Carquinez Straits, where grain could be brought to the docks by both rail and water. Most of the grain moving down the rivers was carried on large barges, which were towed by steamers.[11] The scows played a comparatively small but probably not insignificant part in this trade, as they carried moderate loads (50-150 tons) and provided direct service to any spot that was close to a navigable waterway. In many respects scows filled the place taken by today's motor-trucks, for the system of navigable waterways radiating from San Francisco Bay provided a far more elaborate transportation network than did railroads of the day.

Traffic between San Francisco and agricultural regions was not all one-way. Scows carried bulky items of all sorts to outlying communities, and lumber was probably the most

The Hay Wharf on Mission Creek . . . In the 1870s the haymen unloaded their cargo on any wharf they could nudge into. It was the only city business allowed so much informality. Promised a wharf of their own in San Francisco's China Basin, the haymen finally wangled a small pier that jutted out from Pope & Talbot Lumberyard into Mission Channel.

important of these out-going cargoes. As in the case of hay, the scow was well adapted to this cargo, having plenty of clear deck space for the arrangement of the load. Planks and timbers that were not over 30 or 35 feet long were often carried athwartships, for ease of handling, with the ends projecting several feet beyond the hull on either side.[12] Towns like Petaluma imported large amounts of lumber; one lumber company operator there reported having seen 27 scows in the creek at one time, most of them discharging lumber.[13] As in most of the other scow trades, the scow men were their own longshoremen, and had to handle each piece of timber in loading and unloading. Unloading alongside a dock usually entailed waiting for high tide, when the load could be passed easily to the wharf, and it often took more than one tide to put ashore a hard-to-handle load like timber.

Loads were arranged for on a personal, catch-as-catch-can basis, for most of the scows were owned by their captains, the more prosperous of whom might also own another scow or two which would be operated by a crew for a percentage of the earnings.[14] In 1900, for example, 123 out of a sample of 168 scows were owned by men who operated no more than three scows, and about half of the 168 were owned by one-scow men.[15] The small operator had no office other than the cabin of his vessel or the local barroom, which made for rather casual business relationships. For a small percentage of the freight, independent skippers sometimes picked up loads through larger operators, who had more business than they could handle.[16]

After the turn of the century, the big scow outfits were the Piper-Aden-Goodall, Thomsen-Collier (managed by John Erickson), John (Toe-Jam) Olsen, and James Peterson fleets.[17] The Piper-Aden-Goodall and Thomsen-Collier fleets were the largest during the period immediately preceding the First World War, consisting of as many as a dozen scows each and possibly several sharp-bowed schooners. P-A-G operated some of the largest scows on the Bay: the *Mono*, and

sister-ships *Shasta* and *Alpine*, built for the company by Matthew Turner.[18] Olsen and Peterson each ran a half-dozen or more scows, and several other owners operated three or four. The Remillard and the Fortin Brick Companies operated their own scows for a time, some of them especially constructed to withstand the strains of lying on the bottom when loading or unloading a heavy deckload of brick in the shallows at low tide.[19] Many of the brickyards were located along the shores of the bay, and as was pointed out in Chapter II, a large number of scows participated in this trade.

During the 1860s and 1870s, many scows engaged in hauling coal from Black Diamond (present Pittsburg) to San Francisco. The extensive lignite deposits on the north slope of Mt. Diablo were discovered in 1859, and by 1867 large quantities of coal were being mined.[20] River steamers often coaled at Black Diamond, and nearly every day several scows unloaded coal at San Francisco.[21] The coal was of very poor quality, but it was able to compete with imported coal until the middle 1880s, when increased mining costs plus low prices on foreign coal, resulting from the large number of grain ships that brought coal as ballast to San Francisco, combined to drive it from the market. Mt. Diablo coal sold in San Francisco for about $6.50 per ton during the 1870s and for around $5.50 per ton for the river steamers at Black Diamond. Flour mills, sugar refineries, and other industries needing steam used this coal.[22] The decline of the Mt. Diablo mines did not mean the end of the coal trade for the scows, however, for it was still necessary to distribute coal imported from the Northwest, England, and Australia to the various users around the bay and upriver.

Cord wood, too, was transported in large amounts by scows. As described by Captain John Leale, the down-river freight from Sacramento during the 1860s "was usually cord wood, which the schooner captains would buy from the wood barge-men. Wood sold to bakeries and woodyards, and for $5.00 to households. These barges were owned and operated by California Spaniards. They were towed to a point on the

Part of the Job . . . *The crew of* Wavelet *doubles as longshoremen. Every sack of grain loaded by hand had to be unloaded individually at the destination.*

National Maritime Museum, San Francisco

Upper River by the light draft sternwheelers of the California Steam Navigation Company and after loading would drift with the current to Sacramento."[23] Large loads of cord wood were piled on the scow's decks nearly as high as the hay loads, and as with hay cargoes, it was necessary to reef the sails *up* so the booms could clear the load.[24]

Another industry in which the scow participated was the salt trade between the Alameda shore and San Francisco. During the 1850s some people began gathering for sale in San Francisco the salt that accumulated in natural evaporating ponds along the east shore. Regular salt *making* was started, using these ponds, in the early 1860s. By the early 1870s the salt business was quite large, with landings and warehouses established at Mt. Eden, Union City, and other places. Steamers carried the salt out of the larger landings, and schooners stopped at the smaller landings; freights for the short haul to San Francisco were around $1.25 a ton in 1871.[25] Artificial ponds were built as the demand for salt increased, and scows were engaged in this trade up through the days of the motor scows.[26]

31

The scow captain was his own cargo producer in the sand, gravel, and shell trades. Here, again, the design characteristics of the scow were most desirable, as the flat bottom and shallow draft permitted the scow to be beached on an even keel. When the tide ran out and the crew went out to dig sand or shell, the deck was not so high above ground level that loading was excessively difficult. Sand and gravel banks were located up the Sacramento, San Joaquin, and Napa rivers and in the south bay. The best oyster-shell beds were also in the south bay. Wood Island, in the Sacramento River, was noted for producing any grade of sand, from "plaster sand" to "top sand," and one of the best gravel deposits was on the Napa River.[27] During the later days, about the time that scows were beginning to be motorized, sand and shell were loaded by pumping equipment, but during most of the sailing era shovels and wheelbarrows were the only special equipment used.

Scows often were used for odd jobs, as when the *Blairmore* capsized in San Francisco Bay in 1896. The ship sank on her side and was covered at high water; a scow schooner was moored nearby to serve as a lightship until the vessel could be raised.[28] The scow *Catalina* was fitted as a salvage vessel and aided in raising the *Blairmore*.[29] Scows also served another special purpose admirably, occasionally chartering out to groups for parties on the bay, particularly on the Fourth of July excursions.[30]

The San Francisco scow was suitable for the transport of nearly any type of bulk goods, and its special characteristics — flat bottom, broad and clear deck, and special fittings — made it particularly desirable for the transportation of some goods. Their flat bottom gave the scows a shallow draft and made them cheap to build, their moderate size encouraged a wide field of operation and made them easy to handle with a crew of two, and the wide area and great diversity of their operations encouraged decentralized ownership. It is not surprising that the scow was usually a one-man business, for the low cost of the vessel was within the means of any man who could save a little money, and larger-scale operators had no great advantage over the owner of a single scow. Only a few companies operated such a large number of scows that the owner, or owners, devoted themselves to the operation of the business rather than to the navigation of a scow.

Chapter IV

William Letts Oliver photograph,
National Maritime Museum,
San Francisco

Master Mariners' Race of July 4, 1891, Off to a Slow Start . . . A light breeze carries a good-sized "outside" schooner, possibly John F. Miller, *towards the Hunters Point stakeboat. The barkentines* Makah *and* Wrestler *are already away, while under the shadow of Telegraph Hill, eight other competitors are making their start.*

William Letts Oliver photograph,
National Maritime Museum,
San Francisco

Deepwater Barkentine versus Snag-jumper . . . _The big square-rigger's skysail and royal gave her an edge in the light airs at the start, but now the barkentine will do well to hold her weather berth against the handier scow in the foreground._

Master Mariners' Regatta

The sailor likes a boat that sails well, and ever since there have been sailing craft, sailors have pitted their boats against others in trials of speed. The desire to produce faster boats often has influenced the evolution of local sailing craft types. In workboat design, speed is rarely the most important desirable quality, yet, other things being equal, the better boat is the faster boat. Thus, racing has been and still is a standard against which sailing craft and sailors are measured. The standard may be a false one. The development of interest in racing may easily pass beyond the healthy stage of encouraging better sailing qualities in vessels, without undue sacrifice of other qualities, into a stage of cut-throat competition in which seaworthiness, cargo capacity, comfort and handiness are delivered up to speed, and where the seaman becomes thoroughly specialized as his boat. Yet, however much a sailor may despise racing machines, particularly workboats-turned-racing machines, he is still proud of the speed of his boat and enjoys a little honest competition.

So widespread and continuous is this competition that the description of any sailing vessel demands some comment as to how she fared when sailing on a tack with some other vessel of her general proportions, or what her time was on a run from one well-known point to another. In San Francisco, as in other seaport towns, general reputations for speed were supplemented by more formal trials of occasional match races between rival craft. However, regular racing between large numbers of sizable boats apparently was unknown on the West Coast before 1867, when the Boatmen's Protective Association staged a regatta for workboats on July 4th.[1] The

following year, when the Boatmen's Protective Association became the Master Mariners' Benevolent Association, the regatta became a regular Fourth of July event on San Francisco Bay, awaited with keen anticipation.

The Fourth was a great day in San Francisco during the 1870s and 1880s; the whole population of the city turned out to celebrate the holiday in one way or another. Parades and speeches took up the morning, and the afternoon was devoted to picnics, watersports, or any other divertisement congenial to the participants. Explosives were distributed more widely than they are today, and liquor was cheaper. A combination of the two produced a lively holiday, spattered with shootings, bombings, fires, and other catastrophes. The Master Mariners' Regatta was a happy addition to this medley, for it provided an afternoon spectacle for those who might wish to enjoy the fresh sea breeze from the top of Telegraph Hill. Indeed, thousands climbed the hill and lined the wharves to watch the bay and coastwise freighters take a day off to try their speed around a tough twenty-mile course.

Modern yacht racing is about as popular a spectator sport as rifle shooting. To watch a vast number of small craft, divided up into groups of nearly identical boats which are quite indistinguishable from one another at any distance beyond five hundred yards, is a diversion only race committees can enjoy. (Even this breed is not exempt from ennui and eyestrain.) Although it may be as much sport to sail a thirty-foot sloop as an eighty-foot schooner, it is certainly not as much sport to watch one. But more than thirty-foot sloops raced in the days of sail workboats.

The morning of the Master Mariners' Regatta during the

1870s might find a five-hundred-ton barkentine, complete with skysail yard and figurehead, tacking about between Alcatraz and the waterfront in preparation for the race. About her would be "outside" schooners, measuring up to a hundred or

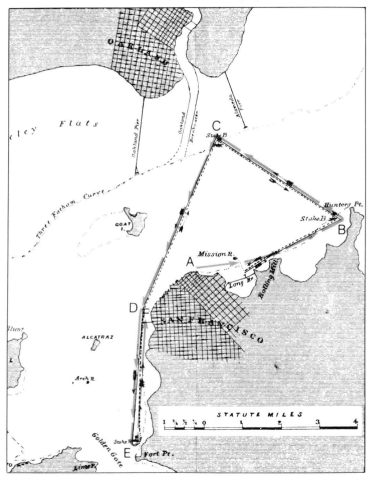

Master Mariners' Course, *superimposed on the 1877 regatta course of San Francisco Yacht Club. Starting from the foot of Market, to Hunters Point, to stakeboat C opposite Oakland and back towards Telegraph Hill, to the stakeboat at Fort Point, and home. The crowds on Telegraph Hill had the chance of seeing the big ships start, middle and finish.*

more feet in length, sixty-foot scow schooners, and little sloops, no bigger than those which race on San Francisco Bay today. From the top of Telegraph Hill, the spectator was able to follow the course of the entire race — from the foot of Market Street to Hunters Point, across to Oakland, and then to the Golden Gate. The last leg of the race, from the Presidio, past Black Point, and down to the waterfront, was very exciting for the spectator, as the large vessels sailed quite close to the shore. Not only was the race itself colorful, but all of the shipping in the harbor and most of the wharves were decorated with flags and bunting.

So that they might enter the regatta, coasting skippers who were members of the Master Mariners' Association made a special effort to have their vessels in port over the Fourth, and scow and coastwise men alike saw that their boats were freshly painted and in their best trim. The little-used fisherman staysail was broken out, for there would be more than enough crew members to handle it. Large parties went with the racing craft, and sometimes as many as a hundred ladies and gentlemen would clutter the decks of a large schooner. Beer by the keg and a goodly supply of stronger spirits were carried to spur on the crews of the winning boats and raise the flagging enthusiasm of the losers. The committee followed the race in chartered tugs or sternwheelers, with a load of guests and a well-stocked commissary. The Master Mariners were out for an afternoon's fun when they raced.

Yet the competition was often very keen, for the prizes were much sought after. Vessels were divided into as many as six classes: round-bottomed schooners, scow schooners, and sloops — each of the first and second class. The first prize in each class was the Association's coveted "Champion" banner — a red silk flag trimmed with gold, with a game cock in the center on a white field and the word "Champion" emblazoned across it. Second and third prizes were similar banners, in different colors. Fourth, fifth, sixth and seventh prizes usually were awarded, depending upon how many were racing in the

National Maritime Museum,
San Francisco

Granger *and* **Garibaldi** *Square Off... On the port tack for the long beat to Fort Point. The wind has picked up and it is still anybody's race.*

various classes, and ranged from silver goblets and marine glasses to gold sleeve buttons and cap insignia.[2] In addition, prizes often were awarded for the fastest time in the fleet. In 1869, for instance, the harbor master offered a silver medal, the sheriff an American ensign, and a wood and coal yard operator promised the winner the choice of either a cord or a ton for the galley stove.

Considerable money sometimes was wagered on the race, both by competitors and spectators. Not only were bets made before the race, but also during the race, again showing that bystanders had little trouble following the various fortunes of vessels, even at a great distance. Betting occasionally added an edge to the contest, as happened when the scow schooner *Champion* failed to enter the 1869 regatta. *Champion* was considered one of the fastest boats on the bay, and a story was bruited about that her skipper, Amos Hewett, had not raced her for fear of losing. Captain Clemmens, of the scow schooner *Tartar*, after making this observation in a barroom following the regatta, was challenged by Hewett to a match race the next day. A two-hundred dollar side wager clinched the bargain. *Champion* won the race, proving the folly of Clemmen's wager more than the speed of *Champion*, for *Tartar* was not a notably fast scow.

The Master Mariners' Regatta was sailed by time, the minute and second noted as each vessel crossed the starting and finish lines. Entries would mill around between Alcatraz and Telegraph Hill before the one o'clock start. When the gun was fired, they would make for the line, off the Market or Howard Street wharf. As each vessel made its own start, the competitors were strung out for about four miles. With thirty or more vessels racing, many of them measuring up to several hundred tons, it would have been extremely hazardous to start together. Although a contemporary painting shows a pack of schooners rounding the mark bunched like a dinghy fleet,[3] such a scene in reality probably would have caused more marine disasters than there were in the regatta.

Even so plenty of casualties marked this rough and ready competition. In the heat of the race, men like the scow schooner captains, who fought for the right-of-way up the narrow reaches of Petaluma Creek with lumps of galley coal for ammunition, did not always firmly adhere to the strictest rules of the road.[4] While protests were not unusual, disqualifications were unprecedented. Added to the normal hazards of carrying a full press in San Francisco Bay's strong summer breeze, collisions resulted in many withdrawals. During the 1871 regatta, *Colonel Baker* lost her topmast, *U.S. Grant* lost her bowsprit, and *Mary Nelson* her centerboard; *N. L. Drew* fouled a ship at anchor and tore her main, later colliding with *Champion*. The only protest came from the skipper of the "plunger" *Challenge*, who withdrew from the race complaining that the Fort Point stakeboat was under sail.

In 1877 a lively dispute took place when the crew of the schooner *Galatea* insisted that the schooner *Big River* deliberately had rammed them as they tacked, even though there had been plenty of room for *Big River* to clear them. *Galatea* made up for the injury by winning the next regatta, held in 1879. More immediate retribution came to the crew of *Good Templar* in 1872, when they stubbornly claimed the right of way against *Fairy Queen* and lost their jibboom in the resulting collision. Except in such cases of swift and impartial justice, protests were left to be settled on Judgment Day.

The course usually sailed by the Master Mariners started from the center of the waterfront and ran to a stakeboat off Hunters Point, thence to a boat off the Oakland Bar. From the Oakland Bar to the Fort Point stakeboat was the longest and roughest leg of the course, about eight miles and a dead beat in the usual fresh westerly. Even with the ebb tide, as many as ten tacks were required, and against a flood tide, many more. The last leg, from Fort Point to a finish line off Meigg's Wharf or the seawall, was downwind. The total length of the course was about twenty nautical miles, although it might have been more or less, depending on the location of the start and finish and the position of the Hunters Point stakeboat. The latter easily could have been moved a mile or two up or down the bay to provide a shorter or longer course, as inclination or weather dictated.

The winning time was usually between two hours and fifteen minutes and two hours and forty-five minutes. The best time in the scow schooner division was in most cases only about fifteen or twenty minutes slower than the best time in the fleet, even though the long windward leg was certainly not to the scow man's liking. The only victory over the entire fleet won by a scow was in the 1870 regatta, when the scow sloop *P.M. Randall*, A. L. Hewlett master, won a slow race in the time of 2:50:57. She defeated two rather notable vessels, however, one of them the *Caroline Mills*, an outside schooner known for having her greatest beam at the main riggings. *Caroline Mills* had won the previous year's race and would turn in the best time on the two following years. The other vessel *Randall* defeated was the plunger *Gazelle*, a sloop which compiled the most outstanding record in the history of the Master Mariners' Regatta.

Gazelle was built in 1868 in San Francisco. She grossed fourteen and one-half tons and was thirty-six feet long, with a beam of fifteen and one-half feet, and a depth of four feet, three inches.[5] In the 1869 regatta, *Gazelle* had nosed out the much larger *P. M. Randall* to win in the sloop division, only to lose to the scow-hulled *Randall* in 1870. In 1871, *Randall* did not race, but a new rival was entered for the swift *Gazelle* — *Challenge*, a slightly larger plunger of the same beam and depth but four feet longer. As in the case of the much-copied *Randall*, *Gazelle* was not to be beaten by an imitation. *Challenge* withdrew from the race, and *Gazelle* won in her class. The next year she handily beat *Challenge*, which finished this time, in a race on which there was wagered quite a bit of money. She won again the following year, to earn permanent possession of her "Champion" banner. Not allowed to compete for the prize in 1874, she sailed anyway, and swept the fleet, defeating

by eight minutes in a fast race her old rival, *Caroline Mills*, a heavy weather boat.

The scow schooner *Rosella* was the only other vessel ever to win permanent possession of the "Champion" flag. Sailed by Louis Morrill, the sixty-foot scow won in her class in 1869, 1870 and 1871. Forty years later, *Rosella* still carried a broom at her masthead, commemorating her victories in the Master Mariners' regattas.[6] *Rosella*, and the other fast scow schooners, never equalled the times set by the big round-bottomed schooners, but they did surprisingly well. *Rosella* always beat as many, or more, of the sharp-bowed craft as beat her, and in 1884 the fast scow schooner *Nettie* ran only eleven minutes behind the winning outside schooner *General Banning*, a vessel twice her size. Peter Demming, who owned and sailed *Nettie*, made the most of her speed; before the race he had her hauled out and her bottom greased, a not uncommon practice and one which indicated the keeness of the competition. In many cases, scows defeated yachts, which sometimes entered the regattas even though they could not compete for the flags.

In all of the regattas, the vast majority of entries were bona fide cargo craft, and the Master Mariners' Regatta seems to have acted as a mild spur to the construction of faster vessels, as attested *Champion*, *Champion II*, *Master Mariner*, *Gazelle*, and *Challenge*. A class of "racers," however, never developed. Small plungers, which were a "yachty" type of craft, came closest to being a racing machine of vessels belonging to association members. It never became necessary to develop strict measurement rules governing entries in the regatta. Rough division into classes, with no limits to the sail carried, except in the case of square sails, was the only "rule" ever used. As a result, members were sometimes annoyed by the entrance of yachts in the races, although, by custom, outsiders were allowed to race with the fleet. It was only when a yacht placed first that any loud grievances were voiced. The howls were loud in 1873, when the crack schooner-yacht *Minnie* took the honors, if not the prizes. Nevertheless, the Master

James Byrnes *Breaks Out Her Pennant . . . One of the smartest scows in the race, the* James Byrnes *breaks out her ensign, her Master Mariners' pennant and her little-used fisherman staysail to compete in the 1884 regatta. The crowd aboard the ferry in the background watches her working to windward, trying to reach Fort Point on this tack.*

William Letts Oliver photographs,
All views, National Maritime Museum,
San Francisco

Mable Gray *and Friends . . . The thousands of San Franciscans who enjoyed the race from Telegraph Hill were matched by the hundreds who managed to bring top hats and picnic baskets as guests on the big schooners like* Mable Gray.

Last Leg . . . Scow Schooner Broadguage *sailing in Class B, attempts to catch up to the large "outside port" schooner just ahead.* Broadguage *will probably succeed as scows were exceptionally fast off the wind. The pair have rounded the finish line off Howard Street Wharf.*

Winning the Pennant . . . General Banning *is being driven hard. A make-shift patch covers the hole ripped in her foresail by* Robert & Minnie's *jibboom. In spite of this handicap,* General Banning *won her race, beating the schooner* Lizzie Merrill *by one second.*

Mariners found little reason to object to yachts entering the races, for the yachts rarely made the best times. It is doubtful if any yacht on the coast could have beaten the beautiful *General Banning* or the best of her contemporaries, and in the later races the yachts were conspicuously absent.

The climax to the regatta was the annual Master Mariners' Benevolent Association Ball, during which the prizes were awarded to the afternoon's winners. The ball was a grand affair and often sported such decorative touches as the illuminated and perfumed fountain in the middle of the dance floor which highlighted the 1875 ball. Upwards of one thousand dollars worth of prizes were distributed each year, and nearly every crew which entered the race received some sort of prize. The larger number of prizes was given partly as an award for turning out for the race, for it was the committee's desire to encourage as many contestants as possible.

Toward the end of the 1870s, enthusiasm for the regatta declined somewhat. Whereas in 1875 forty-two vessels had entered the race, only twenty participated in 1877. No regatta was held in 1878, and after 1879, when only twenty-two entered, the race was dropped and was not revived until 1884. The 1884 regatta produced one of the best races in the history of the event, but in 1885 interest fell off again. No more regattas were held until 1891, when an untimely resurrection turned up only fourteen contestants.

Popular interest in the regatta also declined after the 1870s. Not only did fewer people watch the races, but waterfront interest in the Fourth of July as a whole declined. Less effort went into the decorations, and fewer ships were decked with flags. Instead, interest shifted to rowing races, and crowds thronged Long Bridge, across Mission Bay, instead of Telegraph Hill. It may have been just as well that enthusiasm for the Master Mariners' Regatta flickered out. Although first-class racing and a great show disappeared from San Francisco Bay, the single-minded enthusiasm which would have been necessary to have kept the event alive also would have precluded the most engaging quality of the contests: their spirit of casual amateur competition, in which a good time was the most important element of a good race.[7]

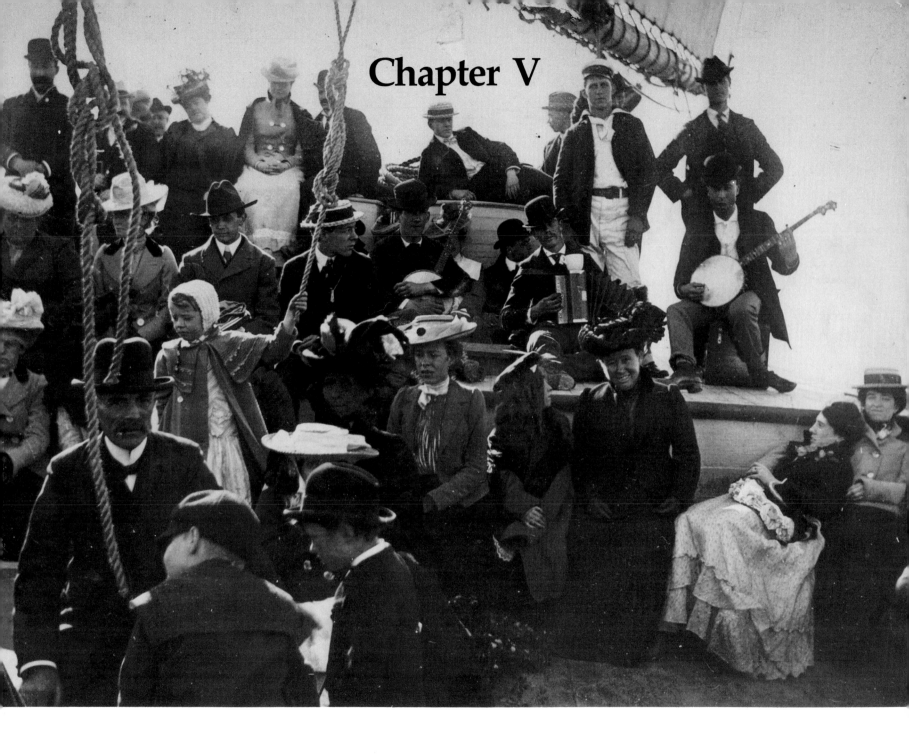

Chapter V

Butchertown Neighbors & Friends Of the Waack's . . . In about 1910, the Charles W. *sets off for the annual spring excursion to picnic in Paradise Cove or McNears Point in Marin, where they might stay overnight.*

Both views,
National Maritime Museum,
San Francisco

Previous page

Launching **James F. McKenna** . . . *"When he built the* McKenna, *my uncle (Charles Waack) said, 'Oh, that's too big — you'll never get enough hay to load it,' and that's why this* McKenna, *the weighmaster, said 'If you'll name the boat after me, I'll be able to get you work.' Well, my father (William Waack) said he never got him any work, but he never needed it anyway . . . [The* James F. McKenna *could carry 825 bales of hay that weighed 200 lbs. each, or 80 tons of hay stacked five tiers of bales above and two below.]*

"At the time of the earthquake we lived aboard the McKenna. *We had two staterooms, one on either side of the eating cabin. There were two bunks in each; my bother and I were in the same bunk. It had a head, which was quite something for those days, most of them didn't . . . We loved the boat. My father and uncle had excursions all of the time. They had big picnics,*

and sometimes we stayed overnight at McNears Point, and slept down in the hold, all our neighbors and friends . . . In hot weather they put a galley out on the deck — out in back somewhere. Just a stove. The bucket came over the side and they washed the dishes . . . They didn't drink river water . . . so they carried their drinking water and cooking water with them.

"A lot of the people (in this view) were our neighbors. At this time we lived out in Bayview — we called it Butchertown. Many scow schoonermen lived there because at that time, if it was high tide at three in the morning, they walked down to the wharf and there was no transportation problem."

Mrs. Arend Horstmeyer, niece of Charles Waack,
interviewed in 1967 by Anita Mozley.

Tule Sailors

The men who sailed the scow schooners were, more often than not, deep-water mariners who had arrived in San Francisco as crew members of foreign ships. A disproportionate number of them, at least toward the close of the 19th century, were of German and Scandinavian origin. Then as now — almost a century later — these peoples made up a large percentage of the world's merchant seamen. Also, during the days of sailing scows, immigration from northern Europe to the United States was heavy (over half a million Germans and Scandinavians arrived here between 1900 and 1905), and the sailor's method of immigration was to jump ship in the port of his choice. Newly arrived seamen naturally tended to follow their trade, and they found life in coastal and inland shipping out of San Francisco far more pleasant and profitable than their previous service in foreign square-riggers.

While the life of the deep-water seamen could be represented by a "typical" career, the diverse opportunities of the inland sailor imposed such little restraint on personal ambition and ability that it probably would be impossible to reconstruct the typical life of the scow schooner man. Some of these men stayed in the scows most of their lives; others went into coastal shipping or back to sea; and, since the shore was always close at hand, many quit the water completely, turning to farming or city occupations. Some never rose above the position of deckhand, while others bought their own vessels, a few of them rising to considerable wealth and prominence — for example, Captain William Matson, who worked on scows briefly, began his own successful deep-water shipping company.[1] But if the lives of the scow schooner sailors took

many directions, life in the scows had its definite characteristics, and these particular qualities are nowhere better illustrated than in Hans Beck's experiences during the last years of the sailing scows.[2]

Born in Denmark, like many of the scow men, L. Hans Beck arrived in San Francisco in a British ship. He had gone to sea several years before he signed aboard the *Blackbraes* as an able-bodied Seaman, and although he was only 17 years old, he found that he was the only certified A.B. aboard — all of the other sailors had lost their papers long before, when they had jumped ship in one port or another. The *Blackbraes* arrived in San Francisco Bay in the spring of 1908 carrying a load of coke for the smelter at Selby plus steel for the rebuilding of San Francisco. At Selby, 16 of her 24 men deserted, but Beck was serving his two year apprenticeship for an officer's ticket and was determined to stay aboard, despite the miserable pay and diet of "salt buffalo" (meat exported from America to England "for ship use only"). However, a friend of Beck's family, who had immigrated to San Francisco some years earlier, had been expecting his arrival and boarded *Blackbraes* with two bottles of scotch and a pocket full of $20 gold pieces. Young Beck soon saw the unreasonableness of his intention to remain with the ship and departed for San Francisco.

Within a day Beck learned scow men made good money, and fellow Danes at the Hay Wharf told him that he might get a job in the Thomsen-Collier fleet. He went to see the manager of the company, John Erickson, who put two questions to him: "Are you a sober man?" and "Can you paint?" Satisfied by Beck's answers, Erickson took him over to Oakland, where he set up charge accounts for him at a grocery and a hardware store, put him in charge of seven schooners lying in the creek, and told him that he would be paid one dollar a day for the next month to clean them up. The vessels were in sorry condition, but Hans set to work, getting up before dawn and turning in long after dark. Erickson had said that he would drop in from time to time to see how the work was coming along, but he never appeared; so at the end of the month Beck borrowed a dime to get to San Francisco and went to the office to collect his pay. Erickson wanted to know, "What the hell are you doing away from the boats?" and "What the hell have you been doing with all that paint?" — it seemed the bills had been coming in.

Satisfied by Beck's explanations, Erickson paid him off and told him to get back to the scows "before the pirates get everything!" It wasn't long before Erickson came over to look at the scows; he was so impressed by their yacht-like appearance that he agreed that Beck might sail aboard the first boat to go out at $40 a month. *St. Thomas* (see pages 65 and 70) was the first scow to leave, and Beck was already aboard when the captain and mate — a pair of Norwegians — rolled aboard, staggering drunk, shortly after dawn. Much to their pleasure, he fixed breakfast for them, but when they expressed their satisfaction with his cooking, he told them that they had eaten the last meal that *he* would cook. Some argument followed, but Erickson had been good enough to tell Beck that an honored scow schooner custom awarded the cook's job to the *newest* member of the crew. Beck stood his ground and maintained his rights, but the Norwegians did not concede the point very gracefully, determining to give him a "rough time" at the next opportunity.

The first voyage was to Milpitas, to load hay. *St. Thomas* arrived there after midnight, and they began to load the hay at two o'clock in the morning. Beck had seen a couple of hay scows going by and thought that it would not take much intelligence to load hay properly. It did not, which was fortunate, as the skipper and mate disappeared, leaving him

to load the hay by himself. The next trip was up Cache Creek to load barley from Rye Island. The barley was piled in 115 pound sacks on the levee, and the Norwegians, stung by Beck's success in loading the hay, put him to work stowing the bags in the hold while they trucked them down off the embankment five at a time, as fast as they could. Beck saw that if he mishandled one bag he would fall behind and never catch up. They loaded about 150 tons of barley (probably a slight exaggeration on Beck's part) into the hold and on deck in one hour, and the Norwegians gave up the rough treatment.

Most of that summer was spent in running up Cache Creek for grain, which they carried down to McNear's dock at Port Costa. Unloading alongside the wharf, the sacks were handled by longshoremen. In the fall they brought hay down from Cache Creek to Stump's wharf at San Francisco's Butchertown. But Beck had not forgiven the Norwegians their unsociable conduct, and he decided that one summer and fall with them was enough. Hans Beck quit, although the skipper told him that they were making so much money for the company that they would probably be the last boat to be laid up for the winter and even offered to pool his entire $65 a month salary with him.

Erickson offered him a $50 a month job with Gus Olsen in the *Surprise*, one of the first gas-powered bay freighters[3], but Beck saw little future working in a scow fleet and refused. He moved in with some young Danish immigrants who shared expenses keeping a little apartment at Ninth and Minna, and one of them, who worked for Jack Ortley, said that Ortley needed a skipper for the scow *Champion*. Beck and his friend went down to the Barbary Coast in the evening and they found Ortley in the "Golden City" with a blonde on each knee. Ortley, who ran several vessels out of Alviso and kept a large hay-barn there, only wanted to know whether or not Beck was familiar with the South Bay. When Beck assured him that he knew it like the back of his hand, Ortley offered him $60 a month to operate *Champion* and told him that his young

Gus Lawrence, Scowman at Whiskey Slough . . . *"Six of us went over to the St. Louis Bar on Front Street — 1908 this was. Right off this bark from Boston, with a little money in our pockets, and we had to get rid of it before we did anything else. We bought a whole quarter keg of beer, set it up in the middle of the table. Had it about finished when in comes this man in overalls. He looked like an old spittoon cleaner, and drunk as an owl he was. But he pulls out gold and buys drinks for the house. He wants nine sailors to go up the Sacramento and load hay and work his scows. We all six went — up to one of those big hay ranches. We're supposed to be heaving these 250-pound bales on board, and the old man who owns the ranch comes down and wants to know why we aren't working. 'No wine, no hay!' we tell him. He goes back and brings down wine. When we have one scow loaded, some of us sail with her. We have a barrel of wine on top of the hay, and it's night, so when we come down on the bridge at Rio Vista nobody's got wind enough to blow the horn. But the bridge tender sees us and opens up (not like at Courtland the time we took the bridge right out). Down off the end of Sherman Island the tide changes. Someone threw away the hook — didn't make the line fast, and she was gone. So we turn in anyway, everybody drunk, and we drift up on Sherman Island at high tide. Next morning the cook looks out and says, 'Fine wind, set the sails, boys.' Fine wind all right, but the man can't get her to steer. We're two miles up on the mud."*

Interviewed in 1956 by R. R. Olmsted & Photographed by Karl Kortum
National Maritime Museum, San Francisco

nephew was to be the crew.

The next morning Beck went down to the Hay Wharf and picked up *Champion*. The nephew cooked breakfast, and they took the scow up to McNear's Point to load crushed rock for a road being built from Alviso to San Jose. They loaded during the afternoon and did not reach Hunters Point until after dark. Beck was in fact in unfamiliar waters, for the only time he had ever been in the South Bay was that first trip to Milpitas. Yet *Champion*, like most sailing scows, was not cluttered with navigational aids, such as charts and compass — the skipper was supposed to *know* the bay and rivers.

Up to this point Beck had managed to convince Ortley's young nephew (who turned out to be somewhat older than himself) of his competence. He would not *ask* his crew which way to go. Beck solved this distressing problem by conducting an examination of his crew's ability to handle the vessel by himself. For example, when Beck saw a bewildering string of lights stretching across their course he turned and asked, "Do you know what those lights are for?"

"Sure. That's the new bridge."

"And if you had the wheel, would you know where to go?"

"Right through there." (Pointing)

Ortley's nephew knew the South Bay, and they made the south end without accident. Beck decided to anchor for the rest of the night, instead of trying to find the entrance to the slough in the dark. The dawn found them right off its mouth, which established Beck's ability beyond doubt.

Before long, Ortley offered to operate *Champion* on shares with Beck – one-third to Ortley and two-thirds to Beck, Beck to pay the expenses. This was a hard bargain, for ordinarily the owner paid the upkeep;[4] but Beck hired a crewman for $50 a month, very high wages for that time, and for the next year-and-a-half they spent little time sleeping. *Champion* lifted 100 tons of canned goods at $1 per ton, and they could make about ten trips a month to San Francisco, despite difficulty getting out of Alviso slough except late at night on an ebb tide. Within eighteen months Beck had saved $3700 and was ready to go into business on his own.

For some time Beck had been watching the operations of Charley Robinson, who loaded shell in the South Bay and ran it up to Petaluma. Oyster shell was fed to chickens to produce sturdier egg-shells. The shell beds covered large portions of the South Bay bottom, and Charley would run his scow up on a shell-bank, wait for low tide, run a plank over the bow, and then load the shells by wheelbarrow. Labor — which was considerable — was the only cost, yet a load of shells was worth about $250 at the Golden Eagle Milling Company in Petaluma.

Charley expressed his willingness to part with the "red" *Dora*, and Beck paid cash in full for her. She was called the "red" *Dora*, to distinguish her from another scow *Dora* — the "green" *Dora*. (Scows were almost invariably painted either red or, more often, green.) Robinson arranged to meet Beck in Petaluma, to pick up his clothes and shotgun, and left. When Beck reached Petaluma with his first load of shell, a woman was standing on the dock. She demanded to know where her Charley was, or what Hans had done with him. When he said that he had bought the boat, and showed her the bill of sale, she said, "How could you have gotten a clear bill of sale when Charley owed so much on her?" Beck did not know quite what to do in this situation, but Mrs. Robinson did: she stomped off to swear out a warrant for Charley's arrest. Beck sold his load of shell and went back to Alviso for another, and when he returned to Petaluma, he found the U.S. marshal waiting to "put a plaster on the boat." It turned out that Charley Robinson owed about $700 to the boat-yards, sailmakers, and ship-chandlers; even the saloon-keepers were trying to attach the *Dora*. But the manager of the Golden Eagle Milling Company, recognizing Beck's future value as a hard-working scowman, bailed him out. Soon Beck and "red" *Dora* were back in business.

Hans found hand loading to be much too slow; he was

Serious, But not Fatal . . . The Robbie Hunter *was refloated and operated for another thirty years after this sinking in August, 1905. Note the wheel pulpit detail.*

making little more money than he had hauling canned goods. For some time Ortley had been sending a man out of Alviso every day to gather shell with a tiny barge and pump. The pump would bring up shell all right, but not very much and the shells were very dirty. Nonetheless, Beck followed up the idea, and installed a 10 H.P. engine driving a pump with a 4″ pipe on the *Dora*. In addition, he washed the shells with the discharge from a smaller pump as they passed over an endless belt made of bed springs. The bed springs never worked satisfactorily, and after a couple of years of experimenting Hans replaced them with a belt made of a wire cloth, much like that used for fireplace screens today.

Beck sold shell not only in Petaluma but at Suisun, Stockton, and Sacramento. The run to Sacramento was the most difficult, taking about three days. Below Sacramento is the "headreach," where the channel (looking upstream) bends to the northwest into the prevailing wind. The river is too narrow here for tacking easily, and worse, the tidal effect is not sufficiently strong to ever reverse the current. A boat depending on sail alone could wait quite a while for a shift of wind at this place,

and ordinarily it was necessary for sailing craft to kedge their way upstream through the headreach, which required taking the anchor upstream in the yawl boat and setting it perhaps twelve or fifteen times. The vessel was then cranked up to the anchor with the winch. Sometimes, in the early days, steamers would tow strings of sailing vessels caught in the headreach for a stiff fee.[5] Beck's best chance for a tow was to wait for the *Jas. F. McKenna* to come up, if he knew she was not too far behind. The *McKenna* was in the transitional stage between sailing and motor scow; she towed a 10 H.P. launch, which in turn pulled her through calms and such places as the headreach.

Hans Beck bought *Robbie Hunter* in 1914 and rigged her for the shell trade. The following year he procured a contract from the Union Oil Company paying $400 a month, less expenses, to run petroleum products upriver on a regular delivery route. He put engines in *Dora* so that he could operate her on this schedule. *Dora* would run from Oleum to Martinez and every little landing along the Straits and Suisun Bay, making Pittsburg the first night. From Pittsburg *Dora* would run up river, making some 80 stops a day, as far as Clarksburg, just below Freeport.

Each farmer was equipped with a little Union Oil Company flag which he would set out on the bank, along with a note, if he wanted some kerosene, distillate, oil, grease, etc. On the way back the crew would pick up the empty cans, making Oleum in time to catch the 9:52 train on Saturday night. Standard Oil ran a sternwheeler over the same general route, but it naturally stopped only at the regular landings. Thus, the farmers soon went over to Beck and direct delivery, and after about two years he bought *Andrew Jackson* to help out in the trade.

In 1915, when he was running *Dora* for the Union Oil Company and *Robbie Hunter* in the shell trade (still under sail), Beck built a large shell dredger with the financial backing of the Pacific Guano Company to bring up shell from the Morgan Oyster Company dumps. These shellmounds were located at Ravenswood, Belmont, and Millbrae, and because of the size of the shells (imported oysters) and the way in which they were compacted, ordinary shell-pumping equipment was inadequate. Within a year, the $40,000 dredger, tug, and barges were almost paid for. Beck and the two young fellows he had taken into partnerships to run the dredger were clearing over $1000 a month.

Beck himself worked mostly aboard *Robbie Hunter*. In March 1916 he was loading shell off Redwood City, when his leg got caught in the pumping machinery. Hans' leg was crushed and almost completely cut off. The helpless crew man did not know what to do, so Beck cut off his leg with his pocket-knife and told the fellow to get him to Redwood City. The next month Hans Beck was married.

Beck gave the dredger to his partners, and as soon as he was able to get around again, fitted *Robbie Hunter* with engines. By the end of World War One, the era of the sailing scow was passing. In the years that followed most profitable scow schooner operations employed gas scows. Beck expanded his

shell business, and in 1932 built another dredger and sold his last scow, *Robbie Hunter*.

Hans Beck received the heavy financial backing necessary to expand his shell-pumping operations to such a large scale because he was competent, hard-working, and dependable. Nearly all scow men were hard-working — loafers could not last long in the business. But many scow men tended to cling to the old sailor's habit of going on a monumental binge every time they hit port. Since scow sailors "made port" not twice a year, but twice a week, their capacity was limited only by their income. Most of them lived aboard their vessels and kept up no permanent shore residence; therefore, they had plenty of money for liquor. Probably more scow sailors were like the Norwegian mate and skipper of *St. Thomas* and Charley Robinson, the former owner of "red" *Dora*, than like Beck.

The most notable of San Francisco's scow ports was Mission Creek, variously known as Channel Street, Third Street Channel, or Mission Canal. Captain Fred Klebingat, who arrived there in 1909 at the age of twenty, recalled: "At the end of Third Street there was a narrow waterway, officially named Mission Creek, but I never heard it called by such a refined title. It was an open sewer, a cesspool that emitted offensive odors, especially at low water . . . . We knew what the contents of the creek were! They said that if you fell overboard you'd not last more than two minutes . . . . As bad as the stench was, still this was the busiest place on the San Francisco waterfront. From Pope & Talbot's lumberyard on the north side and the Hay Wharf (angling southeast, off of Pope & Talbot's) steam schooners, sailing vessels and hay scows lined either side of the creek, leaving barely enough space for vessels to be towed down the middle. Ships' crews groaned at the order that brought their vessels here — the escaping gases from the creek discolored the paint of the hulls inside and out. But ships came to Shit Creek in droves to discharge their lumber cargoes, and hay scows came to the Hay Wharf to get rid of their deckloads."[6]

China Basin Reflections . . . *Landfall in sight and not much of a breeze to lift the sail of the* Annie Maria. *Time to light up a smoke and reflect on the day's trip. Hay from Milpitas, brick from Remillard Landing, chicken feed for Petaluma, shingles for Wood Island . . . hire a little steam tug and make it home the easy way.*

Both views, Walter Scott photographs,
National Maritime Museum, San Francisco

Waterfront cafes and saloons clustered around the channel to accommodate the immediate needs of crews arriving and departing from his busy place. Edward Morphy wrote: "Sarcin's Restaurant was on the southeast corner of Third and Berry streets, diagonally across from Caesar Brun's grocery but the favorite feeding place of oarsmen (from the rowing clubs on Mission Bay) and sailors was the chop-house run by 'Johnny Killa-da-fly.' Johnny's chop-house at 808 Third Street, boasted a splendid cooking range with beautiful copper pots and boilers for tea, milk and coffee, rice and vegetables of every kind, so dear to the heart of a bluewater sailor. It was clean as a pin, and was kept along lines then considered uncanny in their sanitariness. Mine host had but three fingers on his right hand, but with these he wagered war intermidable on the flies that were the pest of the place. As soon as a fly dared light on his counter, swat would go the three-fingered fist, while between his clenched teeth, 'Killa-da-fly!' "[7]

A famous San Francisco institution, "the free lunch," made serious inroads on cafe business. With every pitcher of beer a fine spread of pickles, hard-boiled eggs, cheese and corned beef would be within arm's reach at the bar. Perhaps the favorite scow schooner hangout was Tietjen's Bar at Third and King. In their haste to wet their whistles after a hot, dry trip from the hinterland, scow men were known to dash for Tietjen's without bothering to secure their boats properly, and it caused no great astonishment when a scow drifted down on the bridge with the ebb tide.[8] Often, when they planned an early-morning departure, crewmen would spend the whole night at the saloon, and with the growth of the canning industry, tomato juice became a prominent item in the ship's stores.[9]

However, even some long-time scow men were moderate drinkers and the Jennings brothers did not drink at all.[10] In 1864 the elder Jennings, a Mormon, built *Traveler* on Goat Island for his sons, Moses and John. Jennings built his scow upside down with cross-planking, and he forged all the iron

fittings himself (the usual San Francisco scow was planked fore-and-aft on the bottom). Jennings' technique was considered rational enough in the construction of flat-bottomed craft on the East Coast, but it was regarded as just another of Jennings' aberrations by scow schooner men. Isaac and Davis, the other two sons, operated scows at a later date. Isaac had *Lizzie T. Adams* and David had *Adelia Griffin*. John also built *Plowboy*, for his own use, at Oakland in 1876.[11]

Not only were the Jennings brothers non-drinkers but they were also very religious and fairly well educated, which marked them as odd birds indeed among scow men. Moses and John were so religious that when "it came on to blow," they would just throw the anchor over with a short warp, retire to the cabin, and read the Bible. Apparently they trusted God to see that the anchor found the bottom before the scow fetched up against something solid, and it would appear He took care of them, for they operated *Traveler* for many years without serious incident. Moses, who was the skipper, often told the account of their first voyage in *Traveler*: they went up to Sacramento to get a load of hay for a cavalry unit which was encamped near the head of Islais Creek. They got up the creek as far as the present crossing of Alemany and San Bruno (or Bayshore), floating *Traveler* most of the way, kedging her over the mud in spots.

Kedging or otherwise getting over spots where the water was thin or up a channel against an adverse wind or tide was hard work. When it was possible to walk along the banks of a river, creek, or slough, scows were often towed by manpower. This process, sometimes called "jayhawking,"[12] involved pulling the scow by means of a line running from the foremast head to a canvas sling, which the man (or boy) doing the towing slipped over one shoulder and under the other arm.[13] Along such waterways as Oakland Creek and Petaluma Creek, where school-boys abounded, a two-bit piece often saved the crew considerable effort.[14] To give the scow some direction when there was a favorable tide but no wind or when making a dock on a calm morning, it was often necessary to break out the "Swedish towboat" and put a "white-ash breeze" to work by towing the scow with the yawl boat.[15] (See title page photograph.)

Power craft of various sorts were sometimes available to tow becalmed and tide-bound sailing vessels, but these were employed only as a last resort or in the case of urgent necessity — such as to get up the Third Street Channel to Tietjen's Bar — for tow-boat operators charged what they thought the traffic would bear.[16] A calm morning which found a number of scows anchored off the San Francisco waterfront also would find a few enterprising towboat operators cruising about, dickering with scow captains over the price of a tow to the Hay Wharf or farther up the Channel. The tow men started high, but if there seemed to be the slightest chance that a breeze might come up, the scow men would hold out for a lower price. With each cats-paw the price would come down; and the tow-boat skipper who had asked $2.50 might finally bring a string of scows up to the hay wharf for $1.00 apiece.[17]

The sight of scows becalmed in the bay, with their sails hanging lifeless and the crew lounging on deck is remembered by many old San Francisco residents as a symbol of the leisurely pace of a bygone day. While life in the scow schooners could not be aptly described as having been "leisurely," there were certainly times when the pace was slow. A trip from San Francisco to Petaluma, Alviso or Crockett could take anywhere from six hours to a day or two. A record for "leisurely pace" that must have exceeded any set by the scows was established in 1904 by the big "outside" schooner *Excelsior*, which once consumed 16 days in running a load of lumber from Oakland to Benicia.[18] The *Excelsior* fought headwinds, grounded several times; and ran out of provisions. Some of the crew had to put ashore at Rodeo for fresh stores before a fortuitous shift of wind finally sent the *Excelsior* up Carquinez Straits to Benicia.

Scow men passed many pleasant days up the rivers, when the mosquitoes were not so thick that the use of repellents was necessary.[19] They often had time on these trips for some fishing or duck-shooting, and some married men took their wives along once or twice a year on a river run.[20] Friendly farmers sometimes offered a country meal and the blue-water sailor could well envy the plentiful supply of fresh produce available to the scow man. One of the scow sailor's methods of procuring fresh fruit and vegetables was to raid the farms along the river bank. As described by one light-fingered Dane, "often when we came about we would be close enough to the bank of the river to jump ashore. I have often done this and gone up among the gardens along the river and 'hooked' myself a couple of watermelons and then jumped aboard next time the vessel came about on that side of the river."[21]

Though life in the scows was sometimes lazy, and more often hard, at times it could be dangerous. Like any vessel of its type, the San Francisco scow could capsize under certain conditions, and with a high deckload it was apt to become quite unstable. Raymond Stone experienced one accident resulting from overloading in the early 1920s.[22] Stone had recently converted the *Gas Light* to power and he supposed that she would carry a larger load than she had under sail. Above Rio Vista he loaded 800 bales of hay for the Smith Ranch, on Gallinas Creek. During the night, a strong wind came up and *Gas Light* began rolling heavily, throwing bales of hay first off one side and then off the other. Some 500 bales went overboard before she settled down again. Stone also tried overloading the old *War Eagle* with brick. As he sailed alone from Port Costa to San Quentin *War Eagle* started to open up. Since the pump could not keep up with the water, he headed for Napa Creek, the closest shelter. Near the mouth of the creek, she capsized, and Stone had to swim to shore. The next morning he found *War Eagle* had dumped her deck load and righted herself during the night.

War Eagle turned out to be a rather unlucky vessel during her last years: five months before Stone bought her she had sunk in shallow water in the South Bay, far from shore with

Scow Schooners Head Up Mission Creek . . . Nellie Rich *stops Third Street traffic as the bascule bridge makes way.*

Karl Kortum recalls, "My Uncle Bill, who worked on Channel Creek in 1906, remembered the scow schooners and the thirst of their crews. They sometimes made a careless mooring in their haste to get up to the 'Old Corner' and hoist a few steams. Occasionally, when the tide turned, a scow would come drifting down on the Third Street drawbridge with no one aboard. Consternation and shouting from the bridge tender might turn up someone to lasso her before she got jammed in the works." George W. McNear *takes advantage of the channel towboat to bring this heavily-loaded sand scow to berth on the creek.*

Both views, National Maritime Museum, San Francisco

a load of salt, and her crew of five had all drowned trying to make shore.[23] But *War Eagle* was little the worse for the experience, for the salt gradually dissolved and she drifted off down the bay. *Lizzie T. Adams* refloated in the same way after springing a leak while on her way from Alvarado to San Francisco with a load of salt in 1896.[24] In this case, however, the leak was discovered in time to have her towed to a convenient mud flat where the crew got off. Finally, on Christmas night in 1900, *C.L. Place*, loaded with 60 tons of coal, quietly sank alongside the Beale St. wharf while her crew caroused ashore.[25]

Scow schooners sank or capsized usually as a result of poor handling and maintenance, but probably more scow men lost their lives by simply falling overboard than by having their boat sink under them. Night sailing was attended with some danger as were picnics. On special occasions, parties would be organized for a day on the bay. Men and women, wearing their Sunday clothes, packed hampers of food and, needless to say, brought along vast quantities of alcoholic beverages. Someone brought out a concertina, and the broad decks of the scow proved to be just fine for dancing. These outings were sometimes known as "Drowning Parties," because usually somebody fell overboard, and every now and then somebody drowned.[26]

Sailing scows suffered little from fire hazard, except in the vicinity of the Hay Wharf. During a single week in 1896, three fires started there, and one newspaper attributed them to the careless manner in which scow men knocked out their pipes.[27] When the fires spread to the scows alongside the wharf and burned through the mooring during an ebb tide, scows would drift out into the bay and burn picturesquely.[28] The introduction of the gasoline engine greatly increased the likelihood of fire, and during the 1920s and 1930s many scow schooners burned.

The scow man himself had changed by the time the last of the sailing scows was gone. There was little money to be made in the scow trades by the mid-1920s and the men who bought scows and worked in them do not seem to have been as rowdy as those of the early days; or perhaps it was only that sails and rigging formed a more romantic background for lively doings than gasoline engines and exhaust fumes.

Emil Oberg Recalls Scow Schooner Magnolia

In 1973, when he was 86, Emil Oberg recalled his life on board the motorized scow *Magnolia*, with Karl Kortum and David Hull of the San Francisco Maritime Museum.

"I had my seabag, with my spikes and my regular tool sack and some of my sea clothes that I used when I sailed, in the Bulkhead Saloon [in the Audiffred Building, opposite the Ferry Building]. The bags were stacked up at the back of the saloon; they had a rack on the wall that went all the way up to the ceiling. The fellow who ran the Bulkhead didn't charge for keeping your bag there. He figured he'd get it back selling drinks.

"I was having a drink and a fellow came along and said to me, 'Why don't you go in a scow?'

"What the hell is a scow?" I said.

"Oh,' he said, 'you'd be surprised. Don't think because they look funny that they can't move. . . . So he introduced me to this little stout fellow, Sorensen was his name. 'Why don't you come along with me?' he said, 'I'll give you a good job.

"When I got my bag down, Sorensen picked it up and threw it on his back. I staggered along behind him; we'd both had quite a bit of liquor in us. We were making for Berry Street [Mission Channel] where the scow was lying. She had just been unloading brick. The name of the scow was *Magnolia*. That was in '08 or '09.

"There were three of us aboard beside Sorensen, the skipper. The last man aboard was the cook. . . . I said, 'I don't know a damn thing about cooking.' 'I'll show you how to cook,' the skipper says. 'In the morning you make biscuits. Every morning. And if you want to keep it on hand, you contact some good barkeeper that you know and you'll be the whiskey man too. But he's got to have perfect whiskey. You take two gallons a time.'

"... On my first trip on *Magnolia* we took a load lumber up to Stockton. On the way down we stopped at Antioch. We figured the tide. We would load sand on the high tide. Stick her right into the bank, run a 14-inch plank out and load her up with 'hill sand.'

"... When we came off San Pablo Bay, if it was calm and we didn't want to just lie there, we'd start poling. We had two long poles — about 16 or 18 feet, and a few inches in diameter. I'd take my pole on one side and the other guy poled on the other side. It was an unmarked channel. But the skipper, he knew the channel well so we wasn't pushing against mud, we were pushing against hard bottom.

"Push with your shoulder and once you got her going, you just kept walking. Put down the pole and push and walk, push and walk, going up Gallinas Creek. We'd pole for a good mile till where the shores come together like, then you generally got a little land breeze. You didn't need much sail to go up the creek then. That was about the end of the creek anyway when you got to the brickyard.

"Once you got there, the Italians would load the bricks on board. They would be running the wheelbarrows right into one of the kilns that was cooled off. They usually piled up the bricks when they emptied the kiln . . . I seen bricks so hot that they were pretty hot on your hand.

"... Then we ran down to San Francisco, down to Third and Berry Street. Third Street Channel was a famous, filthy creek. . . . I remember one rainy night we came sailing in there. It was pitch dark and raining. I got ashore and took the stern line. Didn't have time to make fast, but I took a round turn and held her there until she stopped, then when I had enough slack, I made fast. All the other guys . . . went below.

"... I stepped on a spike and the spike broke and down I went in the creek. Pitch dark. I hollered. They never heard me because they were down in the cabin already.

"Well, here was a kid with a raincoat and a bundle of newspapers, selling to the scowers. When he heard me hollering, he took a peek down and saw me hanging onto the piling, so he hollered to the fellows. They came out and got a rope on me and hauled me out . . . And I had to strip right there aft and get off all my clothes and get some buckets of fresh water and wash myself down. That's the only way I could get a bath after that terrible stuff.

"... *Magnolia* was the best paying scow in the bay. I figured on an average of $100 a month — clear money. That was good money in those days. You got $25 shipping out on a deepwater square-rigger. The skipper of the *Magnolia* never missed a stroke. A load coming and going all the time. Moving night and day. . . . We had a lot of respect for Sorensen. We knew he was an ambitious guy and he wanted to put out, too. If you want to make money, you gotta put out. So that's the way it was. . . ."

Chapter VI

Karl Kortum photograph,
National Maritime Museum, San Francisco

The Gasoline Scow . . . Chugging down Petaluma Creek, engines installed and mainmast removed, Matilda *has become independent of wind and tide.*

Matilda, *Loaded with Poultry Feed in Petaluma, 1938 . . . The following year she was sold to Ortley Brothers at Alviso to go into the shell dredging trade. Although Captain Gus Olsen kept her very smart and shipshape until her last days, she wound up abandoned on the mudflats at Alviso a few years after this view was made.*

Karl Kortum photograph,
National Maritime Museum,
San Francisco

The Motor Scow

Emil Munder, who built the last of the sailing scows, *Edith*, in 1906, had already built, four years earlier, a schooner-rigged vessel of semi-scow form called the *Surprise*. John Erickson used her for "outside" runs, and she was fitted with two gasoline engines.[1] Thus, *Edith* was already something of an anachronism at the time of her launching, for a variety of dependable marine engines were on the market after the turn of the century. San Francisco became one of the centers of marine engine construction.

During the early years of the century, the Union, Atlas and Hercules engines were developed in the San Francisco Bay area, and Carl Riott, who built the Empire and later the Standard engines in the East, was from San Francisco.[2] These early marine engines were very large and heavy — the 20 H.P., two-cylinder Empire, for example, turned 400 R.P.M. and weighed about 1500 pounds — but they quickly developed a reputation for dependable and economical operation.[3] Scow operators soon saw that the increasingly cheap and dependable gasoline engines offered considerable advantages over wind-power and after 1910 sailing scows rapidly were converted to motor-vessels.

One of the first power installations in a scow was in Jack Ortley's *Champion*, and consisted of a single 85 H.P. engine driving on the center-line. But as *Champion*'s depth of hold was only four and one-half feet, the large screw required by the big engine was almost out of water when the vessel was light. In this condition she was unable to breast even a moderate tide or current,[4] and Emil Munder repowered her with a pair of 30 H.P. engines swinging smaller propellers. The *Pike Country*, another early motor-scow, suffered from the same difficulty.[5] The engines were usually of 20 to 40 H.P. and were placed in either the cabin or the hold.[6]

The transition from sail to power happened very rapidly. In 1914 the Petaluma newspaper reported that *Anna Aden*, a scow familiar to Petaluma residents, "created a sensation" when she chugged up the creek under her own power, using neither sail nor tow.[7] By 1920 there were at least 38 power scows on the bay, while some 28 still operated under sail, but by 1925 only four of the sailing scows lacked power.[8] In about ten years the sailing scow had become a rarity.

One reason for the rapid shift to power certainly lay with the ease in which the scow could be converted. The engine beds, shaft log and struts were cheap and easy to install in the scow hull. Engines could be picked up cheaply if the owner did not insist on a matched pair: *H. Eppinger* had a Union and an American-Monovalva and *Robbie Hunter* had a 20 H.P., two-cylinder Corliss and a 60 H.P., three-cylinder Imperial.[9] Sometimes the owner would put one engine in the scow and add the other when he had the money to buy it.[10] The tall pilot house which characterized the motor-scow was not an absolute necessity and was not excessively expensive to build anyway. As can be seen in the accompanying photographs, the usual scow schooner conversion also involved cutting off the bowsprit and mainmast. The foremast and boom were left in place to facilitate cargo handling, and the original steering gear and tackle were used. So the changeover to power did not necessarily involve a large immediate cash outlay.

Most of the scows converted to power were old vessels. In 1925, 38 of the scows listed in the appendix appeared in *Merchant Vessels of the United States* as motor vessels, and almost

Roger R. Olmsted Reconnoiters the **Charles W.** . . . . *The wreck of* Charles W. *is beached at Dutchman Slough in the San Joaquin delta country. Her bow transom had been sliced open to accommodate a marine railway for hauling out small craft. The old scow schooner was thus altered to a cross between a floating drydock and a World War II landing craft with a bow*

ramp. Roger Olmsted, then Curator of the Maritime Museum, rowed up for a look as Karl Kortum took this view.

Karl Kortum photograph,
National Maritime Museum, San Francisco

***Scow Schooner* Undine *on Launching Day, 1902 . . .** This view of her stern shows the planking to good advantage. One of Anderson's larger scow's,* Undine *was handsomely fitted inside and out.*

A Prime Example of a First-class Power Conversion . . . *Shown here in 1936 by a San Francisco lumber dock,* Undine *has the typical raised pilot house reached by ladder.*

one-third of these were over fifty years old. At the same time, many of the newer boats had disappeared from the list. Because a power vessel 65 feet or more in length was required to carry a licensed engineer, many scow owners preferred to operate shorter boats. Older vessels were converted more often to power than newer scows, because of the generally larger size of the scows built after about 1890. Of the 38 scows mentioned above, 23 were under 65 feet in length, nine of them measuring between 64 and 64.9 feet. Needless to say, many of these vessels measuring a few inches under 65 feet had been cut to that length when the engines were installed. *Mary*, for example, was cut down from 72.5 to 64.4 feet, *Theodore Roosevelt* from 77 feet to 64.2 feet, while *Adele Hobson* and *Carrier Dove* were pared down only a few feet to get under the limit.[11]

Old *Granger* was a more ambitious rebuilding project. She was so rotten in 1901 that the *Crockett* was built to use her rig. *Granger's* hull was procured by Frank's Tannery at Redwood City in 1909 and completely rebuilt. Frank's employed a

number of scows to bring tanbark down from the Northwestern Pacific railhead at Tiburon and to carry spent bark back to San Francisco to be used in the production of white lead. *Granger* was hauled out on a ways right at the tannery, and the rebuilding resulted in an entirely new vessel, the *Grace & Amy*. She followed the same general lines as *Granger* but had a "V" bow and two 60 H.P. Atlas engines. *Grace & Amy* not only carried a cargo of tanbark but towed a barge or two, thereby replacing about a dozen sailing scows.[12]

Probably 60 or more scows were converted to power at one time or another, but it does not appear that more than about 40 power scows were in use in any one year.[13] During the 1930s the number of scows in use declined very rapidly, and by 1940 very few still were operating. This change, only less rapid than the switch from sail to power, seems to have been caused more by the falling off of water shipping in favor of land transport than by the rise of other types of water transportation such as the tug-and-barge. Cargoes which had formed the backbone of scow operations — brick, lumber, hay

On-Deck, Looking Forward on **Undine, 1936** . . . *Her powerful cargo gaff is for loading lumber.*
Bow-view of **Undine** *(below). She measured 78 feet long and 27 feet across, with a depth of 6.3 feet.*

Both views, Smithsonian Institute, Washington, D.C.

and grain — came to be handled largely by truck; the scows offered something very close to door-to-door transportation, but the trucks furnished the real thing.

As with the sailing scow, many motor-scows were lost to the hazards of navigation or to the ravages of old age. But the motor scow was also subject to abandonment for economic reasons, and the danger of loss from fire was greatly increased by the presence of gasoline. Quite a few scows burned during the 1920s and 1930s, such as *Port Costa*, which burned in the south bay,[14] and *Ellen*, which exploded near McNears Point in 1927.[15] A third, *Annie*, struck a mudbank at the entrance of the San Rafael channel, whereupon a bottle of alcohol used for priming the kerosene stove fell from the shelf and spilled onto the lighted stove. The fire spread to the engine compartment, and *Annie* and her cargo were a total loss.[16]

Some scows were sent from San Francisco to other ports for various purposes, as the cost of building new hulls increased and the value of scows declined. The *Mary*, for example, was refitted during the 1930s with refrigeration equipment and sent to carry clams from Lower California to San Diego. *Albion, Mono*, and *James F. McKenna* also went to southern California, and *Ellen* was patched up in 1931 and went to work behind the dam at Grand Coulee.[17]

The situation for the skipper in the general freight business during 1920s and 1930s was summed up by "Scow Pete" Hanson, owner of *Jas. F. McKenna* during this period. It was a matter of picking up "cargoes of hay, grain, lumber, feed, and anything what came along."[18] *McKenna, Charles W., Hermine Blum* and a few others were kept going during the war years by the army but later sold to other ports or abandoned. *Matilda* was one of the best-kept scows during the late 1930s when Gus Olsen ran her to carry general cargo to Petaluma. When his sight began to fail around 1939, he had

Roger Olmsted Demonstrates Winch Operation . . . *"That was their navigation, that winch. I've seen it so the barrels on each side were so worn that they had holes in the cast iron, and the gear teeth were as thin as paper."*

Captain Volney French

Karl Kortum photograph
National Maritime Museum
San Francisco

Traveler, *Built in 1864, Dredged for Shell in the 1940s* . . . *Her steering mechanism was documented by Karl Kortum in the 1930s, "The 'barn door' rudder of a scow schooner was pulled from side to side by a wheel rope that led in through sheaves in the transom and was wrapped around the wooden drum turned by the steering wheel. The rope was long so that on the occasions when the wheel was raised on a 'tabernacle' so the helmsman could see over the hay load, more of its length could be paid out. To give better purchase to the wheel rope, a short iron monkey tiller was attached to the after edge of the rudder. In the case of the ancient* Traveler *from Civil War times this fitting is absent and the rudder itself has been extended."*

Karl Kortum photograph, National Maritime Museum, San Francisco

trouble navigating the creek without running into the bank, so he sold *Matilda* to Dave Crowley; she wound up in Jack Ortley's collection of rotting scows in Alviso.[20]

The shell-pumping business kept many scows going up through the 1930s, but the superior dredging equipment, such as that used by Hans Beck, kept the price of shell low. Ray Stone operated *Traveler* up to 1940, "wheeling shell" — running up on shell banks as in the days before the pumping equipment — but this was a very marginal sort of operation, as were all of the scow trades by this time.[21]

In 1955 *Alma* was still in operating condition, but at points around the bays and along the banks of sloughs and creeks, more than a dozen scows were lying on the mud in various stages of disintegration.[22]

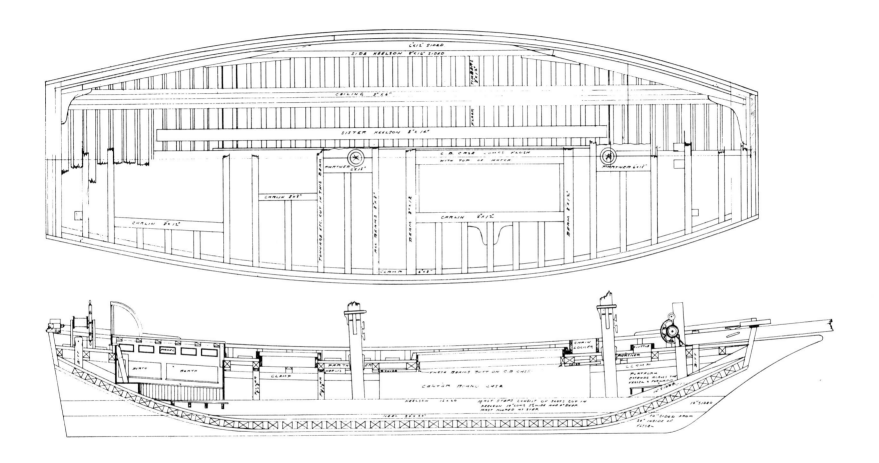

Chapter VII

SAN FRANCISCO BAY SCOW SCHOONER
ST. THOMAS
BUILT 1868

No. 23506 — GROSS TONS 62.47 — NET TONS 59.36
LENGTH 71.4 — BREADTH 25 — DEPTH 5.5

PLANS PREPARED BY J. PORTER SHAW FROM MEASUREMENTS
MADE ABOARD VESSEL WHEN ON MARINE RAILWAY

J. PORTER SHAW COLLECTION,
SAN FRANCISCO MARITIME MUSEUM

Lines of St. Thomas by J. Porter Shaw . . . *The most authentic plans of a scow schooner presently known to exist are those of* St. Thomas, *made by Oakland lawyer and maritime antiquarian J. Porter Shaw. Shaw seized the opportunity when the vessel was hauled out and on a ways to be converted to a barge to make his measurements. This was in the early 1920s and* St. Thomas *had never been motorized.*

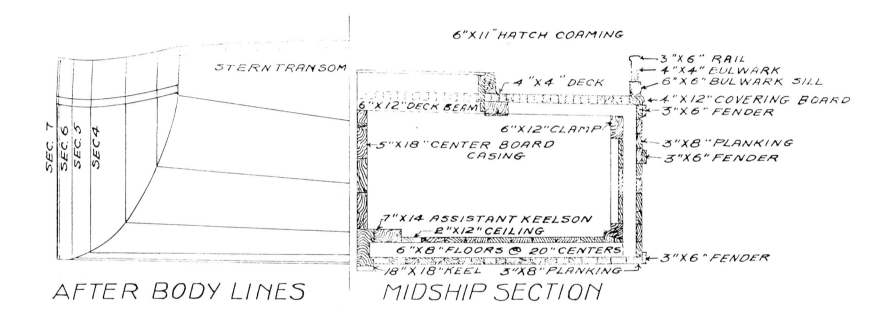

6"X11" HATCH COAMING

3"X6" RAIL
4"X4" BULWARK
6"X6" BULWARK SILL
4"X4" DECK
4"X12" COVERING BOARD
3"X6" FENDER

STERN TRANSOM

6"X12" DECK BEAM

6"X12" CLAMP

5"X18" CENTER BOARD CASING

3"X8" PLANKING
3"X6" FENDER

SEC. 7
SEC. 6
SEC. 5
SEC 4

7"X14 ASSISTANT KEELSON
2"X12" CEILING
6"X8" FLOORS @ 20" CENTERS

3"X6" FENDER

18"X18" KEEL   3"X8" PLANKING

AFTER BODY LINES   MIDSHIP SECTION

Crockett — *Midship Section and After Body Lines* . . . *The San Francisco Bay scow schooner* Crockett *— Plan and Profile are shown later in this chapter. Designed and built by the Munder Brothers in San Francisco in 1901,* Crockett *measured 70 feet 2 inches in length, 25 feet 6 inches in breadth over planking, with a depth of hold at 5 feet 3 inches; her gross tonnage was 63 and net was 44 tons.*

Design & Construction
San Francisco's Bay Scow Schooner

The design and construction of the San Francisco Bay scow schooner, while in no way startling, differed in many respects from that of eastern, southern and Great Lakes scows. Whatever may have been its ancestry, the San Francisco scow was in its details a strictly local type. The great majority were built in about the same way, and the scow schooner *Crockett*, shown in the accompanying drawings, was typical of her type. Built in 1901 by Emil Munder for John Erickson, *Crockett* measured 65 feet long on deck, with a beam of 24.2 feet and a 5.3 foot depth of hold. She was slightly larger than many of the earlier scows but considerably smaller than large scows such as *George W. McNear, H. Eppinger, James F. McKenna, Mariposa,* and *Undine*; all were built in the first two or three years of this century.[1]

The only really unusual departure from normal scow building practice shown in the *Crockett* plan is the slight "V" in the after sections, but Emil Munder, who built her, told the author that he could not recall putting any deadrise in her after sections. Any V in the sections would not only entail a departure from the usual design but also cause considerable difficulty in building, since the standard practice in the fore-and-aft planked San Francisco scow was to run the floors in one piece the full width of the craft, except, of course, in the way of the centerboard trunk. In positioning the top and floor timbers, which together make up a frame, the timbers were rotated on their longitudinal axis so that one of the faces came to bear flush with the side or bottom of the vessel respectively.

As can be seen from the plans, *Crockett*'s bottom, in profile, was flat for about half of the boat's deck length. The sail plan

of "Mr. Rowe's Scow Schooner" shows a rocker to the chine for the entire length of the vessel. *Crockett*'s bottom was typical, while Mr. Rowe's scow may have been of a more or less experimental type. Mr. Rowe's scow was built by the Hall brothers, who came to San Francisco from Cohasset, Maine, and later moved to Puget Sound where they achieved wide fame as shipbuilders. They may also have built the scow *Cohasset*, which was another unusual scow in that it had rounded bilges.[2] In this case the frames were probably of more traditional construction with bevels cut on their face to take the run of the planking. In some scows, the upward turn of the bottom was easier than in *Crockett*.

The sides in all of the scows seem to have been plumb, though photographs and even personal observation of the hulks give the illusion of considerable tumble-home to the sides near the bow and stern. Side planking was made up of a half-dozen or so wide planks with "stealers" worked in at the bow and stern to accommodate the sheer of the vessel. Most of the scows had a pleasing sheer, and the author has seen pictures of few that had a completely straight sheer, although the scow sloop shown on page 14 was very nearly flat on deck. The deck usually was crowned slightly. While some of the scows were nearly rectangular in plan, most of them were much narrower at the transoms than their greatest beam. The narrower transoms were believed to improve the sailing qualities of the scows;[3] *Albertine* had very narrow transoms and was reputed a fast sailer,[4] and the *Nettie*, which was also quite narrow at the ends, proved her superiority by winning first place in the scow division in the 1884 and 1885 Master Mariners' regattas.

William Munder, who built more scows than any other San Francisco boat builder, believed that the greatest beam should be placed well forward, with the after transom narrower than the bow transom, this being the general formation of the better swimmers among the fishes.[6] J. S. Nichols, who built *Albertine* and *Nettie*, as well as many other scow schooners, seems to have preferred to place the greatest beam amidships, or a little abaft, if *Albertine* and *Nettie* be typical examples of his work.[7]

The midship section of *Crockett* on page 66 shows the scantlings fairly well. As can be seen, the keel ran the full length of the flat part of the bottom. The heavy timber on top of the stem piece, called the "anchor stock,"[8] was double, and joined the stem firmly to the keel. There was some variation in the forward timbering of the scows; sometimes the stem was scarfed into a single "anchor stock," with the foremast stepped on it instead of on the stem piece. Whenever possible, the floors ran right through holes cut in the keel, but in the way of the centerboard case they were boxed into the keel as is shown in the *Crockett* midship section. In plan, this assembly appears below.

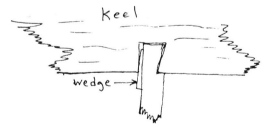

The box was cut wider than the floor, and the half-dovetail cut into the box by means of the dry wedge, as shown. These dry wedges were also driven from each side along the top and one side of the floor that ran clear through the keel, and when they swelled they must have wedged the floors into the keel under very great pressure.[9]

The keelsons were in different positions in many of the scows, and *Crockett* was not unusual in this respect, except that the bilge keelson (knuckle keelson) appears to be notched at its upper inboard corner. This detail is probably in error, as the bilge keelson often consisted of two timbers, a smaller one on top of the larger one. This gave the appearance, in section, of the keelson shown for the *Crockett*. Sometimes another keelson was placed midway between the keel and the chine. The longitudinal timbers often were much heavier than those in the *Crockett*. In *St. Thomas* (see plan), the keel was 24 inches square, and *Robbie Hunter* had bilge keelsons 10 inches by 20 inches laid on the flat.[10]

Frames had a shoulder cut in them to bear on the floor, and they were spiked and bolted to the floor timbers.[11] This method of assembling floors and top timbers into a complete frame was perhaps the most distinctive feature of San Francisco Bay scow construction. No other domestic scows were framed in this manner. Although requiring very complex joinery between the ends of the floors and top timbers, it completely eliminated the need to cut the typical bevel required on the face of frames for vessels with round or V bottoms. Posts shown in the *Crockett* drawings between the bilge keelson and clamp do not seem to have been typical. Deck beams in *Crockett* were bent to the crown of the deck. A more standard practice was to cut the upper edges of beams to the crown in the way of the hatch and the masts, where the deck load was carried, using the lighter bent beams toward the bow and stern.[12] Sometimes heavy posts were used to support the corners of the hatch,[13] and the bulwarks were often tumbled-home to minimize damage in rolling against docks. The centerboard trunk shown in the *Crockett* plans is typical. Scows ordinarily had 3 × 8 ceiling, which was used for strength, being carried right out to the ends. Bottom planking was applied in parallel lengths with the outer shim edge being nibbed into a wider plank set at the edge of the bottom and shaped to the body plan contours. Most scows were ceiled fore and aft on the bottom and sides. Some had vertical ceiling on the sides.

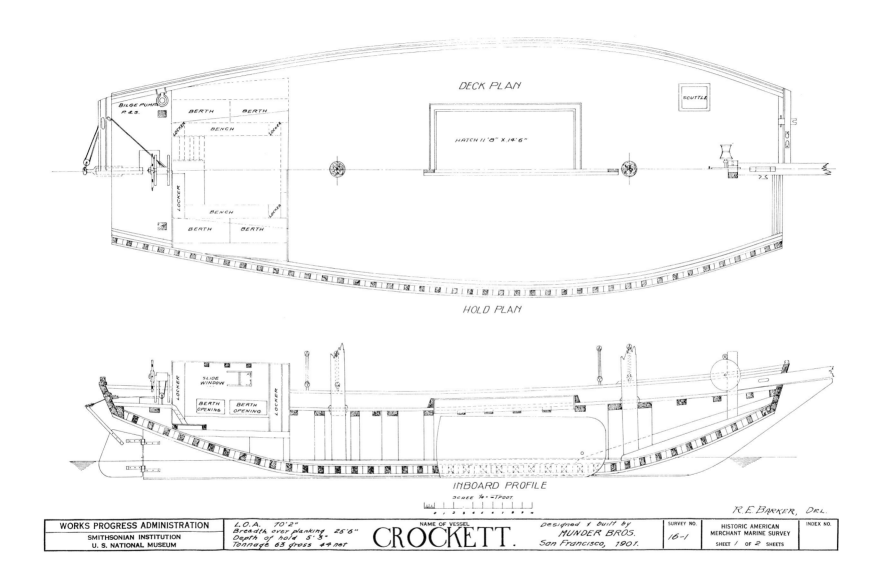

DECK PLAN

BILGE PUMP P & S.

BERTH | BERTH
BENCH
LOCKER | LOCKER

SCUTTLE

HATCH 11'8" X 14'6"

BENCH
BERTH | BERTH

HOLD PLAN

SLIDE WINDOW

BERTH OPENING | BERTH OPENING

LOCKER

LOCKER

INBOARD PROFILE

SCALE ¼" = 1 FOOT

0 1 2 3 4 5 6 7 8 9 10

R.E. BARKER, DEL.

WORKS PROGRESS ADMINISTRATION	L.O.A. 70'2"	NAME OF VESSEL	Designed & built by	SURVEY NO.	HISTORIC AMERICAN	INDEX NO.
SMITHSONIAN INSTITUTION	Breadth over planking 25'6"	CROCKETT.	MUNDER BROS.	16-1	MERCHANT MARINE SURVEY	
U. S. NATIONAL MUSEUM	Depth of hold 5'3" Tonnage 63 gross 44 net		San Francisco, 1901.		SHEET 1 OF 2 SHEETS	

These charts are reproduced from Historic American Merchant Marine Survey, "Crockett," Smithsonian Institution, Washington, D.C. Survey 16-1, above is Sheet 1.

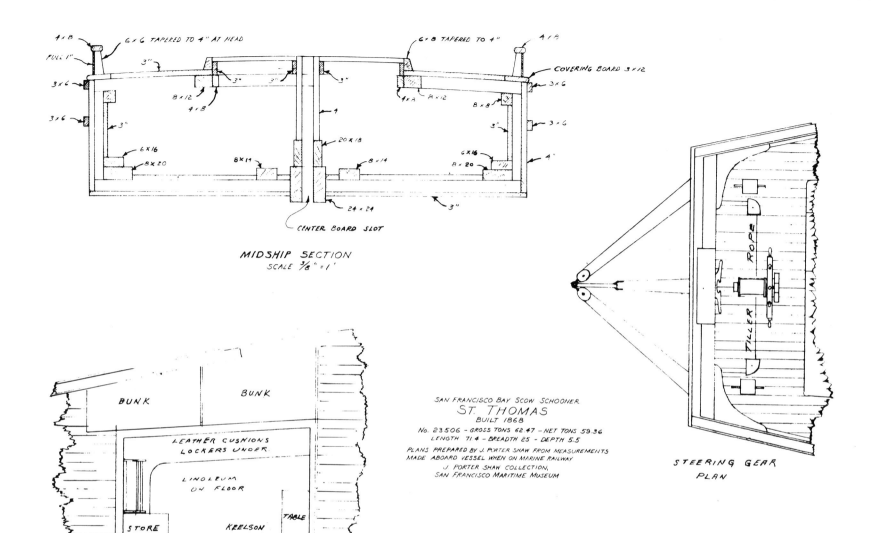

MIDSHIP SECTION
SCALE 3/8" = 1'

1×8 · 6×6 TAPERED TO 4" AT HEAD · 6×8 TAPERED TO 4" · 4×8
FULL 1"
3"
COVERING BOARD 3×12
3×6 · 3"
8×12 · 4×8 · 4×8 · 8×12 · 8×8 · 3×6
3×6 · 3"
6×16 · 8×14 · 8×14 · 6×16 · 3"
8×20 · 20×18 · 8×20 · 4"
24×24
CENTER BOARD SLOT

BUNK · BUNK
LEATHER CUSHIONS LOCKERS UNDER.
LINOLEUM ON FLOOR
STORE SPACE · KEELSON · TABLE
FRONT OF LOCKERS & TI.
LOCKER
BUNK · BUNK

CABIN PLAN

SAN FRANCISCO BAY SCOW SCHOONER
ST. THOMAS
BUILT 1868
No. 23506 – GROSS TONS 62.47 – NET TONS 59.36
LENGTH 71.4 – BREADTH 25 – DEPTH 5.5
PLANS PREPARED BY J. PORTER SHAW FROM MEASUREMENTS
MADE ABOARD VESSEL WHEN ON MARINE RAILWAY
J. PORTER SHAW COLLECTION,
SAN FRANCISCO MARITIME MUSEUM

ROPE · TILLER

STEERING GEAR PLAN

Contrasting **Crockett** *and* **St. Thomas** ... *"Although constructed nearly half a century apart, the hull form and construction techniques employed are quite similar. The two vessels are of almost identical length and proportion. This serves to illustrate that by the turn of the century (and the approximate mid-point of the San Francisco Bay's scow's history) the model had developed very little, and had matured and stabilized in the form shown in the* Crockett *plans. The significant difference lies in the size of the scantlings (timber) used. In 1868, when the St. Thomas was built labor and materials were cheaper so we have much heavier material, more closely spaced frames — and all around massive feel to the vessel's frame."*

Notes by Randolph Biddle, scale-model builder.

The *Crockett* plans show most of the rest of the construction and scantlings rather clearly, and it is useless to try to go into too much detail because of the numerous small variations among scows. Many scows were more heavily built, although 3-inch planking seems to have been almost universal except in "log-built" scows, like *Alma*.

Another unusual construction feature of the San Francisco Bay scows was the fore-and-aft planking. According to Chapelle, scow "construction requires cross-planking on the bottom; longitudinal planking almost invariably adds greatly to the cost and labor of construction."[14] Some of the San Francisco scows were cross-planked (all of the log-built scows were cross-planked by necessity), but most of the bay scows like *Crockett* were longitudinally planked. The *Historic American Merchant Marine Survey* drew plans of *Mary*, one of the cross-planked San Francisco scows. Her wide planking was 6×12, laid on edge and edge-bolted, hence "log-built." She used eleven 8×10 or larger keelsons, and while her bottom planking was only three-inch, some of her bottom ceiling, also laid athwartships, was as thick as six inches.[15]

Mary was built by the Munders, and Emil Munder agrees with Chapelle that the cross-planked scow was cheaper and stronger for the same weight. Such a design was certainly much simpler than the fore-and-aft construction, for no floors were used with the cross-planking. Frames also were unnecessary, except for widely spaced posts to stiffen the sides and support the clamp. Bottom planking of the fore-and-aft planked boats had to be steamed because of the sharp upward bend toward the ends, and outboard planks had to be cut and fitted to the curve of the sides. In the cross-planked boat steaming was unnecessary, and the ends of the plank could be cut off to the curve of the sides after planking.

While the *Historic American Merchant Marine Survey* reports that very few scow schooners were log-built,[16] Emil Munder says that this construction was not too unusual; it was employed when the owner wanted a cheap, strong boat. It is hard to see why the cross-planked construction was not more common, indeed, not universal. Perhaps there was some objection to the cross-seams in regard to speed, an idea which has had considerable prevalence. One objection to cross-planking was that when the scows grounded, or lay on the bottom at low tide in creeks and sloughs, any damage sustained by the bottom would have been easier to repair with longitudinal planking than with cross-planking. With the former construction, it was only necessary to butt in a new piece of plank to repair the bottom, while damaged cross-planks, important structural members, would have to have been completely replaced.[17] Yet this and other objections seem relatively minor compared to the advantages of cross-planking. It may be that cross-planked scows, being less expensive, earned the reputation of cheapness and therefore most often were built to a boxy big-load-for-cost model which proved dull and unhandy performers.

Mary was an example of this type, and if most of the cross-planked scows were similar, it is easy to see how some ugly associations could grow up around log-built construction. *Mary* had very wide transoms, as can be seen from her photographs, and the plans show that the flat of her bottom was carried to an unusual length. This made the ends turn up very abruptly, a model poorly suited for speed and probably not so handy as one like the *Crockett*. There is no design and construction reason, however, that a cross-planked scow should be built to the model of *Mary*, rather than to that of *Crockett*, as can be seen in the case of *Traveler*.

Traveler was not "log-built," having planking of normal thickness, which permitted the ends to be sprung in more and produced a more graceful hull. But this construction was highly unusual, if not unique, as attested by the fact that *Traveler* is remembered by several of the old scow sailors and builders as the scow that was "cross-planked, upside-down, on Goat Island." This method of scow-construction (cross-planked but not edge bolted) apparently was considered highly eccentric, but it was at least durable, for *Traveler* operated for seventy-five years — probably longer than any other San Francisco scow.

The rig of the scow schooners was quite standardized and shows clearly in some of the photographs. It usually consisted of a main topsail set over the three lowers. The photographs of the Master Mariners' Regatta in Chapter IV show the scows carrying a staysail or "fisherman." The absence of this sail in the other photographs indicates that the staysail was probably set only for racing. The gaff topsail, which could be clewed up aloft, seems to have been carried more often. Occasionally a scow schooner carried a fore-topmast or was baldheaded.[18]

The spar dimensions of *War Eagle*, listed in Chapter II, were probably typical for a scow of her size. The standing rigging usually included a total of eight shrouds, set up with deadeyes and lanyards, and a mainstay, springstay, headstay, forestay and bobstay. The forestay usually passed around a dumb sheave in the bowsprit to a chainplate just above the bobstay chainplate.[19] The lower sails were sheeted to travelers, and in the later sailing scows, a patent shock-absorber sheet horse often was used.[20] Another gadget was even more universal — the jib club traveler seen on the bowsprit of the scow on page 34. Henry Hall's drawing of *War Eagle* shows a similar device. The purpose of this traveler was to allow the jib to lower all the way down without casting off the clew.

The rudder and steering mechanism shown in the *Crockett* plans was common to San Francisco Bay scows, as well as to most of the large East Coast scows.[21] The plans and pictures show the arrangement so well that there is little need for description. This stockless rudder, with its adjustable tackle, would have been hard to improve upon for scow schooner use. It was exceedingly strong, for the rudder was pulled around from the point at which the greatest strain developed, and the steering tackles took the strain rather than the rudder post. The standing end of the tackle was very long, and when the wheel was raised, it merely was necessary to pay out several feet of line from the standing end and make it fast again. A photograph of the scow *Martinez* also shows a stocked rudder, apparently with an inboard steering arrangement. According to Emil Munder, some of the scows had a partial rudder stock which ran through the bottom and ended underneath the deck. This stock allowed the rudder to ride up when the scow was grounded without upshipping. There were no upper rudder hangings when this construction was used, and the lower pintle was extra long.[22]

All scows carried a large winch on the bitts, which was used in hoisting sails, handling ground tackle, cargo, or any other job which might require a heavy purchase, such as kedging off a mudbank. A typical winch is shown on page 84. Another of the standard scow fittings was the diaphragm bilge pump, fitted aft, port, and starboard, as shown in the *Crockett* plans. The suction pipe ran to a point near the chine somewhere abaft the centerboard trunk. The reason for having two pumps on the *Crockett* was that the bottom, being flat, had no sump, and the scow could best be pumped dry by the leeward pump when the boat was heeled. Most scows seemed to have had only one pump with a hole drilled through the keel to allow both bilges to drain.

Scows generally carried a trunk-cabin abaft the mainmast, as in the case of *Crockett* and *War Eagle*. Occasionally, the cabin was under a raised poop, as in the *Undine* (page 61). The *Crockett* plans show a large, approximately square, four berth cabin under the deck. These were the usual accommodations in scows the size of *Crockett*, though there were probably only two bunks in some of the smaller ones. *Undine*, *Matilda*, and some of the other big scows had the cabin divided up into smaller cabins. *Undine*, in particular, is said to have been finished quite handsomely below.[23]

Chapter VIII

Alma *Moving Smartly on San Francisco Bay, Master Mariners'*
Regatta, 1971 . . . The perfect day for the classic race as the wind moves
the mists down from Marin's headlands and fills the sails. The Danish pilot
boat Orn *is at* Alma's *bow and the fishing schooner-yacht* Thales *races off*
her quarter.

Photo first appeared in *Sail Magazine*,
National Maritime Museum,
San Francisco

Hunters Point Boatyard in about 1900 . . .

Alma *Up for Spring Haul Out at Seimer's Yard . . . (below)*
Alma *is on the left,* Express, *on the right, and* Jessie Fremont *is third in line. Fred Seimer is on the capstan at the far right, Fred Seimer, Jr. is third from the right.*

Both views, National Maritime Museum, San Francisco

Alma Sails Again!

In 1955 Roger Olmsted wound up his thesis chapter on "The Motor Scow" with these words, "Today, *Alma* is still in operating condition, but more than a dozen scows are still lying on the mud at points around the bays and along the banks of sloughs and creeks [of San Francisco Bay] in various stages of disintegration." Four years later, at 1:00 a.m., on Tuesday, August 18, 1959, Roger Olmsted, Karl Kortum and Harry Dring floated *Alma* off a bed of mud at Alviso in a rescue operation that required a certain amount of luck, a six foot tide, $500 from the California Department of Natural Resources, and the help of the tugboat *G. B. Marshall*, operated by Lester Peterson who turned out to be descended from *Alma's* original owner.

Alma's history is so ordinary that she may be correctly described as a "typical scow." What is unusual, for a scow schooner, is that her construction site, builder and owners are remembered, recorded and described.

In the bleak Hunter's Point view of about 1900, Fred Seimer's boatyard faced on Hudson Street, between Hawes and Griffith streets. The boatways reached out from a shallow beach, along the line of ordinary high tide on the southern part of San Francisco Bay, just south of Butchertown's slaughter houses. This "nuisance industry" was relocated from Mission Creek, south to Islais Creek—an area remote from the city in 1870.

Fred Seimer's Hunters Point yard was photographed from a promontory of land at about Evans and Hawes, the later site of Christensen and Munder's boatbuilding yards. Anderson's boatyard is in the background of this view, where the little sternwheeler juts out into the bay. The dark stone tower, just visible behind the masts of boats on Seimer's ways, is the

Albion Brewery, sited on a spring famous for its crystal clear water. It was well-known to the coast Indians and is still producing mineral springs water. The stone brewery building still stands at the corner of Griffith and Innes.

Seimer immigrated from Germany in about 1865, where he had been a boss in a Bremerhaven shipyard. He brought his wife and six children first to Tulare County, and then to San Francisco where he worked as a ship carpenter. He borrowed $350 to build his marine ways from a Mr. Hanson who had a hog ranch.[1] Apparently Seimer's yard mostly did repair work; every spring the scows were hauled up, copper painted on the bottom, and made shipshape for the coming season. He is known to have built the scow schooner *Adelia*, named for Fred Seimer's daughter, who later married James Peterson, *Alma's* owner.

Another view shows *Alma* up on the ways, probably for her spring haul-out. *Alma* is on the far left, the scow schooner *Express* is to her right and *Jessie Fremont* is next in line. Olga Peterson Likens describes the scene in the photograph: "This was my grandfather's shipyard and that is my grandfather (Fred Seimer Sr.) on the capstan at the far right. They had a horse on each side of the capstan to pull the boats up. We kids used to jump up on it and get a ride. This was one of my father's boats (*Alma*, to the far left). August Seimer is there (second from the right). He had a shipyard afterwards, too. Fred Jr. is next (3rd from the right). I don't know any of the others. My father, James Peterson, is up on *Alma*, in the middle, wearing the hat. The second from the left could be old Bill Engel; he was always hanging around there. He's 90 years old last September."[2]

Alma was average size (59' long, 22.6' in breadth, measuring 41.76 tons), but somewhat unusual in her construction in that her flat bottom was planked athwartships rather than fore-and-aft. As has been noted in an earlier chapter, *Mary*, built the same year by the Munders, was also cross-planked which Chapelle believed to be cheaper and stronger for the same weight. *Traveler* (1864) was another scow known to have been constructed "cross-planked," but her ends sprung in more, producing a more graceful hull than *Alma*.[3] According to an interview on cross-planking with Harry Dring, "there was somewhat more drag than with fore-and-aft timbers, the lines tended toward boxiness, and damaged planks had to be completely replaced."[4] Olmsted had earlier noted that this type of construction had a reputation for "unhandiness" that kept it from being more popular.

She was built by hand of Oregon pine (Douglas fir), with no knots, supplied by Pope and Talbot lumberyard. C. J. Hendry, ship chandler, supplied her bolts and oakum.[5]

Alma was built by Seimer in what amounted to the Peterson's front yard, and named for James Peterson's daughter who was three years old at the time. If *Alma* was a typical scow, James Peterson was a fairly typical Swedish scowman, but with a better head for business than most, who made a large success of his scow schooner operation. Arriving from Sweden at the age of fourteen with fifty cents in his pocket, he went to work on the waterfront for the scow schooner owner, Lorentzen, and in due course bought his first scow, *Hector*. At one time he had the biggest scow fleet in San Francisco. A list of James Peterson's scows has been compiled from interviews, federal records and notes by Barbara Fetesoff for her master's thesis, "The Scow Schooner *Alma*, 1891-1975." The list is interesting for maritime scholars because it shows the longevity of sailing scows and their gradual shift to motors and final use as barges.

James Peterson's fleet included: *Adelia* (built in 1886, owned by Peterson until 1917); *Alma* (built 1891, owned by Peterson until 1926, sold to Frank Resech for shell dredging and

motorized); *Emily Lundt* (built 1861, owned by Peterson prior to 1898-1918; dismantled and used as a barge); *Excedere* (built 1869, owned by Peterson from about 1898 to 1905; wrecked); *Hector* (built 1858, owned by Peterson until 1886); *Miami* (built 1887, owned by Peterson prior to 1898 until 1917; dismantled for use as a barge); *Pike County* (built 1851, owned by Peterson prior to 1898 and until 1918, motorized 1898; dismantled for use as a barge); *Star* (owned by Peterson from about 1898 to 1917; dismantled for use as barge and sold in 1930 to Purity Spring Water who motorized her).[6]

James's son, Roy Peterson was 75 years old in October, 1975 when he described his life working on board *Alma*. "The men ate well. In the winter, two fifteen gallon barrels were taken along. One contained pickled pork; the other, corned beef. The crew also had cabbage, hard tack, flour to make their own bread and potatoes. There was a stove in the cabin which burned wood or coal (bought from the scows that carried it). The food had to be preserved in winter because trips could be long. Carrying lumber to Stockton in the winter could take six weeks because of the east wind but the trip back might take only a day. The crew could fish for catfish at Crockett and produce or chicken could be bought at farms along the way . . . .

"*Alma* carried a cargo of potatoes and onions, but not fruit. Mostly she carried hay, grain and lumber. Lumber was the big business. It was shipped from the north coast to San Francisco by steam schooners. . . the scows took it up the rivers. There were lumberyards in Rio Vista, Antioch and Stockton. . . *Alma* would dock in San Francisco at piers 40, 46 and 18. Sometimes I would go out and cover the scows when it rained at night . . . . *Alma* was later used as a barge to haul fertilizer from Butchertown [Hawaiian Fertilizer Company] and salt . . . . Every year in the spring the scows were drydocked and painted with copper paint on the bottom to keep the worms out. The decks and hulls above the waterline were painted, the masts were oiled, and the rigging tarred. After that, the family would take a scow ride with friends to

National Maritime Museum,
San Francisco

Alma *Departs the Hay Wharf at San Francisco, ca. 1890s . . . She sets out across Mission Bay in the light airs of wintertime. She has a partial cargo of baled hay, covered with a tarp in case it rains.*

Alma *as the Last Shell Scow in Petaluma, Chicken Capital of the World, 1937 . . . Seen here converted to gas and used as an oyster shell dredger,* Alma *delivered 110 to 125 tons of calcium rich shell to Petaluma's poultry supply houses to add to the chicken's diet. Avoiding "thin shells" gave Petaluma chicken eggs a superior reputation.*

Jack Eatherton photograph, National Maritime Museum, San Francisco

Paradise Cove, just south of Richardson Bay, in Marin. Occasionally, James Peterson rented out a scow for a ride to Paradise Cove to the Dolphin Club in North Beach. A north wind was blowing and the captain of the rowing club, not understanding the need for tacking, told the scow's captain, 'We want to go over *there*!' "[7]

Alma continued her useful and uneventful sailing career until July 1918 — twenty-seven years, marred only by one collision with the Alaska Packer's steamer *Kvichak* who ran into *Alma* off Stuart Street lumber wharf. *Alma* capsized, losing her entire cargo of sulphate of ammonia — fertilizer worth about $5500 — sustaining about $2000 in damages to herself and losing the citizenship papers belonging to her master, Erik W. Carlson. The tug *Pilot* towed her to China Basin for repairs.[8] In 1918 her masts and bowsprits were removed, and until 1926 she was used as a barge, hauling salt and fertilizer, towed by Peterson's tugboat *Success*.[9] In 1926 *Alma* sold for $10 "and other considerations" to Frank Resech who took *Alma* back to her builders at Hunters Point for repairs and to have two twenty-horsepower Corliss gas engines (taken from the scow *Dora*) installed. Resech converted *Alma* to an oyster shell dredger by constructing a shell bin, 36 by 22 feet on her deck with eight-foot bulkheads above her gunwales. He added a deckhouse with living quarters on top of the trunk cabin, with a wheelhouse above. The wheelhouse contained only the steering gear, her engine controls were below in the engine room.[10]

"Resech and his wife lived aboard *Alma* while she was out dredging. Mrs. Resech would take the helm while her husband ran the dredging machinery. In calm weather they would cruise in a circle at about forty to fifty feet a minute. In heavier weather they would steer a straight course . . . . The shell dredging equipment consisted of a four-inch column pump powered by a four-cylinder stationary gas engine, a revolving trammel, two single-cylinder stationary gas engines, a 45-foot mast, a boom, a belt conveyor, a winch and slip-scraper. The

shells were sucked into the column at the bow and sent up to the trammel where they were rinsed with water supplied by the single-cylinder engine. From there they moved onto the conveyor belt which ran aft, suspended at the end from the boom on the mast. The boom swung athwartships so that the shells were distributed from side to side. The slip-scraper, operated by the winch, distributed the load of oyster shells to the ends of the bin.

"It took about ten hours to pick up a full load. The Resechs would pick up half a load one day and the other half the next, then they would sail to Petaluma to help unload *Alma*. The sleepy but prosperous country town of Petaluma was not only the source of their income but also their home when the Resech family were not dredging on *Alma*."[11] Oyster shell was added to chicken feed for the lime content to create thicker shells.

By 1943 *Alma* was the only vessel bringing oyster shells to Petaluma and she was due for a costly overhaul. Frank Resech was in his seventies and felt he was too old to continue taking *Alma* out everyday to dredge. He sold *Alma* to Peter Gambetta in April, 1943. Gambetta had grown up around boats and owned the Palo Alto Boat Works, working for Anderson and Cristofani during the second world war when dredgers supplied oyster shells for magnesium. Gambetta bought *Alma* for $4000 and then overhauled her for two months at a cost of $13,000.

When Gambetta bought her he discovered *Alma* was hard to steer so he removed the forefoot and modified her rudder. He extended two horizontal outriggers from both sides of the rudder below the waterline and a paneled rubber blade at the end of each side. This formed two tunnels and allowed six surfaces to do the steering rather than two. He replaced her dredging machinery and added a Gray Marine diesel engine that increased her horsepower to 220.[12]

Alma now dredged 55 to 60 cubic yards per hour and took four or five hours to load. From 1944 until 1950 she was the only shell dredger supplying Petaluma. In 1945 she brought

National Maritime Museum,
San Francisco

Alma *Delivers San Francisco Lumber to Petaluma, ca. 1911-1912 . . .*
Redwood and Douglas fir from the Pacific Northwest made its way up winding
Petaluma Creek to become the homes and barns, and fences and roofs for
Sonoma's farming community.

oystershell to Bay Shell of Alviso, a company that provided shell for chickenfeed for the entire state and Hawaii. *Alma* dredged off Bay Farm Island in Alameda for her Petaluma cargo, and off San Mateo shoals or Palo Alto for her Alviso cargo. From 1950 to 1957 *Alma* sold exclusively to the Bay Shell Company. By 1957 Gambetta had finished building a new dredge, *South Bay*, and *Alma* was retired to a mudflat in Alviso.[13] She rested on the mud until August 1959 when her long-about-midnight rescue started her on a third career as the last surviving scow schooner of San Francisco Bay, a National Register Landmark, used to educate generations yet to come with the first-hand experience of San Francisco's own square-toed packets.

Alma's dramatic rescue grew from a seed of an idea contained in a letter Karl Kortum wrote to Scott Newhall (then editor of the *San Francisco Chronicle*) on March 5, 1949, proposing a historic maritime use of Aquatic Park in San Francisco. "San Francisco developed one unique type of craft, the scow schooner, that is completely her own. At one time there were over four hundred of these centerboarders trading on the bay, and their importance in the story of American shipping is sufficient and a scale model of a typical scow is being preserved in the National Museum in Washington, D. C. Before the war there was one [*Traveler*], motorized, that came up Petaluma Creek and she was built during the Civil War. A few scow schooner hulls are still around, and it would not be much of a trick to set the mainmast again and rig a bowsprit and have this quaint old craft riding to an anchor in the basin."[14]

Karl Kortum had grown up in Petaluma on the family farm. It was a town where the sight of scow schooners making their way up Petaluma Creek was familiar and nostalgic, recalling slower pace of life when scows were the everyday workboats, slow moving and picturesque. In the second quarter of the century the grinding of great trucks on freeways replaced the boats winding on backwaters with their calm reflections and independent scowmen making a modest living at an imminently practical way of life. In a way, the scow schooner trade was so ordinary that it existed below the level of most observers' consciousness and could have been as quietly erased from the 20th century as the horse-drawn ice wagon or the family doctor making housecalls in his buggy. It was Karl Kortum's unabashed sentiment for the scow schooners that met Roger Olmsted's love of boats that sail on San Francisco Bay and the men who sailed them. Roger's master's thesis gave the necessary and important scholarly foundation to an all but forgotten class of San Francisco sailing craft.

With Karl Kortum as the founder and director of the new Maritime Museum at San Francisco, Roger Olmsted as the young curator, and Harry Dring as maintenance manager of the historic ships, the three men shared a common vision of ships restored, riding high at anchor at Aquatic Park. They knew with a certainty that time was running out on a great chapter of maritime history, as leftover sailing ships of the world sat in various states of disrepair on backwater creeks and mudflats. It became more and more pressing to save the best of the lot before they were gone. Karl cast around for the best scow schooner.

"I went down to Alviso in 1949 to look at the *Matilda* on the mud flat there, her hull worm eaten through a couple of places. The *Annie L.*, subject of the best 'load of hay' photograph, was nearly in considerably worse condition. The *Hermine Blum* at the mouth of the San Joaquin River, pretty intact on a mudbank across from Antioch, was another candidate." Many weekends were spent trudging through San Francisco Bay's salt marshes and sloughs, shimmying up telephone poles to sight wrecks of wooden hulls, while weighing the possibilities of each derelict boat. But as Kortum recalls, "*Alma* won because she was afloat. I knew *Alma* as a shell dredger, delivering her cargo to Petaluma in pre-war days. She used to lie in the turning basin; a feature was the neat curtains in the windows of the cabin aft. Her running mates still to be found in Petaluma in those days were the *Traveler*, built during the Civil War, and

*Floating **Alma** Off the Mud at Alviso, 1959 . . . Roger Olmsted, Harry Dring and Peter Gambetta tow **Alma** off the mud on a six-foot tide. Gambetta sold **Alma** for $500 to the State of California for her restoration and eventual display.*

Karl Kortum photograph,
National Maritime Museum, San Francisco

the big, well-kept, motorized *Matilda*, carrying grain. The *Traveler* dropped out of the picture sometime before World War II, and when Scott put the *Chronicle* behind the museum idea in 1949 I had an impression that *Alma* had gone to her reward during the five years I was overseas.

"With considerable excitement, therefore, one day after the project for ship preservation was well-launched in San Francisco, I saw a familiar superstructure looming over a Petaluma stringpiece. The view was from Third Street, and I was looking into what had been Capt. Lorentzen's gravel and sand yard. The year would have been about 1950. In some apprehension that *Alma's* deckhouse, mast, and shell bin had been transferred to some less ancient hull, I drove into the plant and looked over the edge of the wharf. *Alma* was still there, under all this, at work, afloat.

"*Alma* thus became the prime candidate for preservation, moving ahead of *Matilda*, which would have required extensive hull repairs because of the worm damage. After this sighting we kept an eye on her — Roger Olmsted, Harry Dring and myself."[15]

Harry Dring recalled the August night when he and Roger Olmsted rigged the towing lines calculated to ease her off the mud, as Karl Kortum photographed the past-midnight operation with the extension flash equipment of his Kodak. "Midnight, Monday, August 17, found us at Alviso with the necessary mooring lines. Peter Gambetta, the former owner met us, and with his power boat, she was successfully floated on a six foot tide at 1:00 a.m., Tuesday, August 18, and shifted to the Bay Shell Company berth in a dredged channel. There was a bay area tugboat strike in progress at the time, and our continuous telephone calls for a tug and rates went un-answered until Tuesday afternoon, when Lester Peterson was reached and made himself available at a competitive price. The arrangement was made for Peterson to meet us at Alviso on the high tide at 2:30 p.m., Wednesday, August 19. . . . On our arrival, the tug *G. B. Marshall*, was standing by and we

left at 2:23 p.m. Our tow to the Oakland Dock and Warehouse Company was uneventful aside from the necessity of running the pump continuously due to heavy leaking, induced by the speed of towing."[16] *Alma's* tugboat rescuer, Lester Peterson turned out to be descended from her original owner. And Alma herself, Alma Peterson Sooman, was rediscovered living out on old "Railroad Avenue" (Third Street) in the southern part of San Francisco, not too far from the early boatyards where the scow schooners were constructed and repaired.

But *Alma* rescued was not *Alma* restored or under sail. Beyond the $500 purchase price, restoration has been estimated at about $22,000 before her masts were put in.[17] It is not possible to be accurate about the total amount of time and care that went into bringing her up to full sail. "In 1964 Haviside Company lifted her out of the water and placed her on the Hyde Street Pier. Due to a miscalculation, the gold rush Tubbs office building on the pier is one of the few land structures that can claim to have the distinction of being hit by a vessel."[18] Although no surveys had been made on *Alma*, the details from the *Crockett, Albertine* and other scows were available from the Smithsonian. Her "hawsepipes are from the *Hermine Blum* and the sheethorse is from *Matilda*. *Alma's* windlass was rusted completely through. The one aboard her came from *Annie L.* . . . Her rigging was made by Jack Dickeroff, master rigger, and park service deckhands in 1967. She was completely restored and back at her moorings in 1968. . . . Henry Rusk, a naval architect, volunteered to design her sail plan and C. J. Hendry, a famous San Francisco ship chandler who had supplied her original fittings, donated her sails."[19]

The Master Mariner's Regatta on May 18, 1969 (revived because of Olmsted's articles in *American West* and *Yachting* magazine) was the happy occasion that saw *Alma* under sail. Harry Dring, who was responsible for her safety and upkeep, wrote, "The race itself went well, the tug *Meridian* picked *Alma* off the pier at a little after 10:00 a.m., Sunday morning and towed her up to Fort Point. During the tow, the crew had been busy getting the gaskets off the sails, and preparing to set the sails. On a signal from Captain Clark, the tug eased back, the line was thrown off, and as the sails were sheeted home, *Alma* sheered away toward Sausalito with everything pulling. The tug dropped astern and trailed along as *Alma* got the bit in her teeth for the first time in fifty years!"[20]

Alma's Winch, ca. 1935 . . . *"Petaluma Creek? That was just a winching job from one end to the other — that's a bloomin' corkscrew going up in there," according to scowman, Bill Werder.* **Alma** *is a boxy scow, about as plain as they come. But it is her very ordinariness that makes it so appropriate that she should represent this entire class of useful vessels that were the workboats of San Francisco Bay from the gold rush "until the 1930s saw the advance of progress — primarily in the form of trucks — drive all but a few of the old scows to the boneyards along the shores of the bay." R. R. Olmsted notes.*

Jack Eatherton photograph,
National Maritime Museum, San Francisco

Editor's Notes and Acknowledgements

*S*cow *Schooners of San Francisco Bay* is published in memory of Roger Robertson Olmsted (1927-1981). It is a tribute to this sophisticated historian that his master thesis, finished when he was twenty-eight years old, should be well-written and so strongly conceptualized as to make it interesting reading to a far wider public than maritime scholars. The original thesis contained twenty-one illustrations and maps; the present volume includes seventy-two, many collected by the author in his position as Curator of the San Francisco Maritime Museum and during the years that followed; he never lost interest in this San Francisco sailing craft. Roger Olmsted published the Master Mariner's Regatta Chapter in *American West*, when he was Graphics Editor in 1964, and in *Yachting*. Later, as Director of Publications for the California Historical Society, he published a pictorial article on San Francisco scows, *The Square-Toed Packets of San Francisco Bay* (1972). Much of this article has been incorporated into this present volume.

Roger was delighted when the California History Center began negotiating in 1979 to publish his thesis as a book. He was most anxious to include the recollections of Captain Fred Klebingat as recorded by Karl Kortum, and the additional information about scow schooner builders that we uncovered working on the historical archaeological reports for San Francisco's sewer project that eventually encompassed the entire waterfront in the 1970s and early 1980s.

In editing and augmenting this manuscript for publication, I have included many additional notes made by Karl Kortum from interviews with scowmen in the years following the 1955 thesis. Karl made generous offers of all his own research notes and fine photographs. He carefully reviewed the manuscript, photographs and captions for possible changes and additions beyond the original thesis materials.

In 1982 I applied to the National Maritime Museum Association for funds to implement the book's publication. The grant was eventually made (1986) entirely through the good efforts of Glennie Wall, Manager of the National Maritime Museum at San Francisco, and for her work I am deeply grateful. She shared my vision of an important and definitive work of San Francisco's scow schooners, so proudly represented by *Alma*, a National Register Landmark afloat at the Hyde Street Pier. *Friends of Alma*, a group of maritime enthusiasts head by Ray Aker and Bill Burgess who had kept watch over the rescued scow, donated their treasury to the project. Additional donations were made by the Sourisseau Academy at San Jose State University, *Latitude 38, Inc.*, the San Rafael Yacht Harbor, and individual members of the Master Mariner's Regatta Association: Jerry and Diane Brenden, Robert Cleek, Frank Court, James Craig, Harry Dring, Clifford Frestad, Edmund P. Halley, Charles Hendrickson, Lawrence Hitchcock, Ken Inouye, Robert Kilian, Neil Moore, Michael Nugent, Walt Petersen, Richard Ponzio, Joshua K. Pryor, Don Sanders, Tom and Lynn Sparks, Peter Stremlau, Frank Tomsick, and William Vaughan.

Our thanks are extended to Seonaid McArthur, past director of the California History Center Foundation, for initially conceiving of this project with the late Roger Olmsted. My special gratitude to Irene Stachura, for her help in locating the original negatives for most of the photographs used in this volume and to the staff of the photographic library and the National Maritime Museum for their efforts to get the highest quality reproductions for this work. Additional thanks to James Delgado, Acting Maritime Historian at the National Maritime Museum at San Francisco, for reviewing the edited manuscript. My thanks to the Bancroft Library for their help in locating additional photographs. A special word of appreciation to Robert Cleek, scow schooner enthusiast, who urged me to continue efforts to fund and publish this book and donated his time, thought and professional services to this end.

Special recognition is due Barbara Joyce Fetesoff for her research on *Alma* in her master's thesis "The Scow Schooner *Alma*, 1891-1975." The interviews conducted for this work added much valuable information to "*Alma* Sails Again!"

Randolph Biddle, certainly one of the most knowledgeable scale-model experts on scow schooner consruction, was kind enough to read the chapter on design and construction and make important comments that have been included in this text.

Finally, *Scow Schooners of San Francisco Bay* was steered through years of fund raising, editing and production by Kathleen Peregrin, Media-Instructional Associate, and Dr. James Williams, Executive Director of the California History Center Foundation. They copy edited the editing, proof-read, made many helpful suggestions, including choice of type and layout, and remained enthusiastic about the project throughout its working process. It is not an easy thing to undertake to edit and publish the work of someone no longer on the scene to answer questions and settle the multitude of small problems that arise, but as editor, and widow, I cannot thank them enough.

Nancy Olmsted
May 1987

Appendix I
San Francisco Bay Scow Schooners and Sloops

T he following list of San Francisco Bay scow sloops and schooners was compiled by the author from photographic evidence, the recollections of men acquainted with the scows, newspaper stories (particularly those dealing with the Master Mariners' Regattas), and United States Custom House documents ("Master Carpenters' Certificates" and "Coasting Licenses"). Unfortunately, few scows were listed as such in their documents. As a result, this list leans heavily upon the recollections of scow schooner men, particularly those of Emil Munder, who started work in his father's boatyard on Hunters Point in 1892 and was engaged in the business of constructing and repairing scows and other types of vessels for the next thirty-three years. As photographs and documents can provide the only absolutely certain identification, there are probably some errors in this list. It almost is certainly not complete and probably omits many scows that did not survive into the twentieth century.

The dates of building, dimensions, and tonnages listed below were compiled from the "Master Carpenters' Certificates" and from the annual *List of Merchant Vessels of the United States*. Names of builders were taken, for the most part, from the "Master Carpenters' Certificates," though some few were found in John Lyman, *The Sailing Vessels of the Pacific Coast and their Builders: 1850-1905* (Maritime Research Society of San Diego, Bulletin #2; reprinted from *Americana*, XXXV, April, 1941), and Caspar T. Hopkins, *Report on Port Charges, Shipping and Shipbuilding . . .* (San Francisco, 1885). Under "dimensions," depth refers to depth of hold (not draft of water).

*Those names marked * were sloop-rigged. Those marked † indicate photographs appear in this volume. For particular page numbers, refer to the index.*

Name	Year Built	Length	Breadth	Depth	Gross Tonnage	Builder
Ada	1890	57.0	19.6	3.5	27.48	William Munder
Ada McCune	1877	58.0	20.0	4.3	36.65	Belden
Addie Gracier	1868	47.5	19.2	3.8	23.64	
Adele Hobson	1904	69.0	26.0	5.2	60.27	Emil Munder
Adelia	1886	48.0	16.5	4.0	31.05	Fred Seimer
Adelia Griffin	1883	52.7	19.5	3.8	27.70	Henry J. Ervin
Agnes	1886	65.0	21.0	4.9	45.00	William Munder
Agnes Jones	1877	48.5	19.2	4.0	24.23	Henry J. Ervin
Alameda	1861	65.0	19.2	4.0	35.53	
Alaska	1867	54.0	18.5	4.1	27.91	
Albertine	1884	63.5	23.8	5.5	50.00	J. S. Nichols
Albion	1886	80.5	27.0	5.0	79.57	Daniel W. Ervin
Alma †	1891	59.0	22.6	4.0	41.76	Fred Seimer
Alpine	1892	82.0	26.0	6.1	95.96	Matthew Turner
Alsen	1903	49.5	17.1	5.0	28.00	L. Korchhoff
Amelia	1877	46.0	20.0	4.1	24.53	Thomas Harvey
America *	1850					
America	1852	61.0	22.0	4.8	39.19	
Amethyst	1883	72.5	26.0	5.7	74.25	Matthew Turner
Anastasia	1870	58.5	22.2	4.3	37.32	
Andrew Jackson	1860	56.0	28.0	4.7	36.62	
Anna Aden	1875	54.0	21.3	4.3	35.10	William Brown
Anna Hermine	1869	70.0	25.5	5.4	66.83	
Annie	1877	57.0	22.2	4.5	41.73	William Munder
Annie E.	1891	71.0	25.6	5.9	72.95	Alexander Hay
Annie Eliza	1884	54.8	20.3	3.8	30.00	John J. Dirks
Annie L. †	1900	65.0	25.0	5.0	60.00	Emil Munder
Annie Maria †	1891	57.0	20.3	4.0	33.88	William Munder
Apache	1864	59.0	20.0	4.4	40.19	
Arthur	1874	64.5	23.5	4.3	48.38	J. B. Piper
Barkis	1864	55.7	16.7	4.6	25.44	
Bedouin	1902	38.0	15.0	4.1	20.00	J. T. Crosby
Benicia	1891	49.6	20.2	4.0	32.00	Matthew Turner
Black Diamond	1861	62.0	22.0	4.7	41.05	

Name	Year Built	Length	Breadth	Depth	Gross Tonnage	Builder
Broadguage †	1878	55.0	22.0	4.3	35.65	George D. Weaver
Brothers	1878	57.0	21.6	4.3	37.76	Thomas Harvey
Brothers	1890	64.3	26.1	5.5	54.89	Alexander Hay
C. L. Place	1858	49.0	20.0	4.4	28.77	
Caesar Bruns	1867	65.0	23.5	4.6	48.81	
Camilla	1875	56.0	21.3	3.3	35.04	O. F. L. Farenkam
Caroline †	1853	62.6	22.5	4.5	34.68	
Caroline Dixon	1878	59.0	22.0	4.7	47.66	George Buckert
Carrier Dove	1864	69.0	22.7	5.0	54.47	Damon
Carro True	1877	47.0	18.0	4.1	21.41	Henry J. Ervin
Catalina	1887	79.5	24.0	6.0	93.32	Alexander Hay
Cecilia Maria	1871	48.0	16.2	3.4	23.22	William Munder
Champion	1867	64.5	23.0	4.5	44.19	
Charles W. †	1902	75.5	27.0	5.6	80.00	
Cohasset †	1887	45.4	16.9	4.1	20.53	
Col. Baker	1864	74.0	26.0	5.4	76.67	James C. Cousins
Columbus	1861	57.0	21.0	4.6	36.33	
Covina †	1902	77.0	28.0	5.8	83.00	R. W. Schultze
Crockett †	1901	65.0	24.2	5.3	62.00	Emil Munder

Caroline . . .

Name	Year Built	Length	Breadth	Depth	Gross Tonnage	Builder
D. N. Darlington *	1900	50.0	16.8	3.6	20.80	
Dora	1874	57.0	21.5	5.1	42.34	J. Peterson
Dora	1884	59.5	23.3	4.8	44.91	Thomas Parkinson
Dreadnaught †	1865	60.0	23.0	4.3	40.00	
Eddy	1873	60.0	22.0	4.2	39.22	O. F. L. Farenkam
Edith	1906	87.0	31.5	6.0		Emil Munder
Edward Louis	1869	70.0	26.0	3.7	46.55	
Elizabeth Greenwood	1877	53.0	27.2	3.7	31.57	Henry J. Ervin
Elko	1867					Patrick H. Tiernan
Ellen	1903	82.0	28.5	4.5	84.00	Emil Munder
Ellen Gunderson	1868	58.5	22.0	4.5	35.84	
Emilie Martin	1872	48.5	17.8	3.3	19.74	William Munder
Emily F. Bichard	1867	62.5	22.5	4.1	39.05	
Emily Lundt	1861	58.3	20.7	4.5	34.24	
Emma †	1876	59.0	22.5	4.7	47.55	Chris Runger
Energy	1870	50.5	18.6	3.6	24.14	
Erma †	1904	82.5	29.2	5.0	94.00	Emil Munder
Eva	1889	64.0	22.3	3.2	36.87	William Munder
Eveline	1876	58.5	23.0	4.0	40.29	
Excedere	1869	58.8	22.0	4.7	43.33	
Express †	1875	60.0	17.2	4.4	33.92	
Fairfield	1855	54.0	19.0	4.0	28.67	
Fannie	1868	66.0	24.5	5.0	61.21	
Fearless	1867	45.0	17.6	3.8	22.03	
Florence Caduc	1878	58.0	22.0	4.3	43.56	George D. Weaver
Fidelity	1885	64.0	23.0	5.0	53.07	John J. Dirks
Fortuna	1855	51.0	14.4	3.7	22.99	
Four Sisters	1895	58.5	20.6	4.0	38.95	Matthew Turner
Fourth of July	1861	60.0	22.0	5.5	49.95	
Frank Lawrence	1886	63.0	24.0	4.5	57.64	Matthew Turner
Franklin †						
Free Trade	1869	86.5	26.4	6.2	91.72	
Garibaldi †	1861	65.3	21.3	4.6	41.79	Stanton
Gas Light †	1874	55.5	22.3	4.4	39.40	Henry J. Ervin
George Washington	1863	50.0	20.0	3.7	23.69	
Geo. W. McNear †	1901	68.0	27.5	5.8		Hans Anderson
Georgia Woods	1868	71.0	21.3	5.4	60.37	
Glory	1863	42.0	14.0	3.5	13.73	
Golden Fleece	1867	60.5	23.0	4.9	47.67	
Golden Gate	1868				71.00	T. J. Thoro
Grace & Amy	1909	65.2	22.6	3.7	48.00	
Granger †	1874	60.0	23.0	4.6	43.08	J. S. Nichols

Name	Year Built	Length	Breadth	Depth	Gross Tonnage	Builder
H. Bendel †	1874	71.5	25.6	5.5	73.70	D. N. Lundt
H. Eppinger	1901	80.0	27.5	6.2	96.00	Emil Munder
Harry †	1876	52.0	19.0	3.5	24.63	J. B. Piper
Harvest Queen	1861	56.0	21.2	4.0	32.44	
Heckla	1874	62.5	22.0	4.6	46.25	O. F. L. Farenkam
Hector	1858	47.4	17.5	4.4	23.91	
Henrietta M.	1895	66.0	24.5	4.9	54.00	William Munder
Hercules	1878	57.1	23.0	4.7	47.35	John J. Dirks
Hermine Blum †	1887	60.2	23.3	4.7	52.71	William Munder
Horace Templeton	1873	48.0	22.2	4.9	42.90	George D. Weaver
Howard	1869	82.0	25.2	4.4	73.39	
Hueneme	1873					William Filken
J. A. Sutter	1850				6⁹⁴/₉₅	
J. J. Stofen	1878	53.0	21.0	4.3	32.35	Charles G. White
James Byrnes †	1870	58.7	21.2	4.0	34.48	
Jas. F. McKenna†	1902	78.0	27.6	6.3	95.00	Hans Anderson
Jennie & Edna	1884	70.0	24.0	5.5	60.60	Matthew Turner
John Frederick	1860	52.9	18.6	4.0	33.95	
John Lambert	1867	52.5	20.0	4.0	30.31	
John Nagle	1867	71.5	24.5	5.6	66.21	
Josie	1869	71.0	24.6	4.5	48.61	
Kate	1851?	34.0	11.7	5.2	17³⁹/₉₅	
Katie Holmes	1875	49.8	18.8	3.8	26.68	J. S. Nichols
Katie S. †	1894	78.5	27.0	5.4	78.00	William Munder
Laura M. Damon	1860	46.0	18.3	4.3	20.51	
Lew Young †	1874	52.0	21.0	4.2	33.19	H. Hansen
Lillian	1888	57.5	27.7	3.5	39.37	William Campbell
Lime Point	1872	49.0	18.0	3.1	19.86	Thomas H. Petersen
Lizzie C. Jurrs	1878	63.0	22.4	4.7	45.83	William Munder
Lizzie T. Adams	1860	52.3	17.0	4.8	26.82	
Lorenz & William	1866	48.0	18.0	4.0	23.09	William Munder
Louise	1870	51.5	20.2	3.8	24.79	O. F. L. Farenkam
McClellan	1855	56.5	15.0	3.9	24.11	
Mabel & Edith †	1867	64.0	23.0	5.1	48.59	Patrick H. Tiernan
Madeline	1873	54.0	20.5	4.5	33.95	O. F. L. Farenkam
Maggie V. Hartman	1867	57.0	22.0	4.4	35.85	
Magnolia †	1869	61.0	22.6	4.5	47.06	
Maria H. Nelson	1864	66.0	22.5	4.2	38.57	
Marie Chevalier	1881	57.5	25.2	4.5	46.47	Charles G. Wilson
Mariposa	1902	78.0	27.0	6.3	95.00	Hans Anderson
Martinez	1876	51.5	17.3	4.2	24.49	George Weaver
Mary †	1891	72.5	24.0	3.5	52.82	William Munder

Harry . . .

Name	Year Built	Length	Breadth	Depth	Gross Tonnage	Builder
Mary A. Fernandez	1869	68.0	24.8	4.6	49.22	
Mary Frances	1877	53.0	21.0	3.7	29.74	John J. Dirks
Mary Frances Cruz	1874	60.0	22.0	4.6	46.41	John Blondin
Mary Gratwick	1858	55.0	18.6	4.8	32.80	
Mary Joseph	1859	47.5	16.6	4.2	23.21	
Master Mariner	1876	56.0	21.4	4.6	39.24	John J. Dirks
Matilda †	1905	79.0	29.0	6.2	102.00	Munder Brothers
May Flower	1888	80.5	26.5	6.2	90.53	William Munder
Melrose	1875	52.0	20.4	3.9	24.66	Henry J. Ervin
Melvina	1889	62.0	22.3	3.2	36.87	William Munder
Merchant	1867	47.0	17.7	3.5	18.58	
Meta	1886	51.9	20.1	3.8	38.65	Henry J. Ervin
Miami	1887	56.0	20.7	4.4	38.11	William Campbell
Mission Canal	1873	62.4	18.0	4.8	47.63	Charles Davis
Modoc	1873	65.0	23.8	4.5	47.99	J. B. Piper
Mono	1904	89.0	31.0	7.2	142.00	Hans Anderson
Montezuma	1884	73.3	26.2	5.9	73.30	Charles G. White
Mose	1875–				73.00	J. S. Nichols
Mountain View †	1867	61.0	24.2	4.5	43.48	

Name	Year Built	Length	Breadth	Depth	Gross Tonnage	Builder
Napa City	1872	68.5	22.0	5.3	46.58	A. Knudsen
Narrow Gauge	1878	47.0	19.0	3.7	23.73	Henry J. Ervin
Natalie	1892	54.0	20.0	3.3	29.88	August Schultze
National	1852	44.6	14.6	3.2	14.86	
Nellie Carter	1867	63.5	23.0	4.8	48.21	
Nellie Rich †	1874	67.0	23.0	4.3	45.76	J. S. Nichols
Nettie	1883	69.0	24.7	5.9	65.70	J. S. Nichols
Nettie Sundborg	1889	74.0	25.4	6.0	66.68	Charles G. White
New England	1850	59.0	11.2	3.9	17.97	
Niantic	1850	51.0	14.1	3.8	21.38	
Nicoline	1888	63.0	19.8	5.8	39.54	L. Kirchoff
Nicholine & Dorthea	1867	50.0	17.0	3.4	19.18	
Nimrod	1853	55.3	16.9	4.0	27.82	
North Beach	1864	66.4	22.6	4.9	46.59	
Olga F.	1905	69.0	26.0	5.0	64.00	Emil Munder
P. M. Randall *					54.53	
P. & R. #6	1870	49.5	20.0	3.7	26.63	
P. & R. #7	1869	49.5	20.0	3.8	24.73	
Paul & Willie	1884	57.8	21.7	4.5	35.66	John J. Dirks
Pike County	1851	66.0	19.5	4.0	35.88	
Pinole	1889	72.0	25.4	6.5	81.64	Matthew Turner
Piute	1874	61.0	23.0	4.6	45.79	J. B. Piper
Plow Boy	1876	63.0	19.8	4.5	39.40	John Jennings
Port Costa	1899	70.5	26.8	5.0	72.00	William Munder
Pride of Wood Island *	1889	45.0	19.1	3.3	19.63	F. C. Lauritzen
Prosperous	1867	56.5	21.0	4.2	34.44	
Rainbow	1862	62.5	22.0	4.8	42.86	
Redwood	1852	55.0	18.8	3.7	26.59	
Redwood City	1902	58.0	20.5	4.0	37.00	Emil Munder
Regina S.	1893	68.0	26.0	5.4	68.99	William Munder
Restless	1875	74.5	26.0	5.7	73.86	S. P. Kimball
Rival	1869	53.5	21.7	4.5	34.74	
Robbie Hunter †	1870	65.6	23.7	5.2	57.36	
Robert Henry	1892	62.0	22.0	3.8	40.06	William Munder
Robert & Jennie	1883	62.5	23.3	5.1	50.38	J. S. Nichols
Rock of Cashe	1862	49.9	19.0	4.0	22.08	
Rock Island	1884	54.6	20.0	3.5	28.93	Henry J. Ervin
Rosella	1868	60.0	22.3	4.3	39.06	
Rough & Ready †	1864	69.0	24.4	5.1	56.00	D. N. Lundt

Name	Year Built	Length	Breadth	Depth	Gross Tonnage	Builder
S. E. Perry	1869	66.0	22.0	4.0	39.44	
Sacramento	1868	86.0	30.0	5.0	130.81	H. Winkelman
St. Thomas †	1868	71.0	25.0	5.0	62.47	
Salamander	1860	52.0	19.0	4.0	30.35	
San Pedro	1887	80.0	24.0	6.0	88.67	Alexander Hay
San Rafael	1890	61.23	23.0	4.5	44.94	John Garcia
Sarah	1877	53.0	20.0	2.9	24.54	O. F. L. Farenkam
Shasta	1892	82.0	26.0	6.1	95.96	Matthew Turner
Solano	1885	74.0	25.0	5.5	66.56	Matthew Turner
Sophie	1883	52.0	18.8	4.4	28.86	Thomas Parkinson
Sophie E.	1895	64.5	22.8	4.5	42.17	O. F. L. Farenkam
Squibob	1860	60.0	18.0	39.18		
Star *	1870	37.0	15.0	4.0	11.62	
Star	1873	62.2	23.0	4.5	47.63	Frederick Russelmann
Sycamore *	1850	56.0	19.0	5.0	34.57	
T. Alonzo	1866	48.0	18.0	3.0	23.14	
Tartar	1868	68.0	24.0	4.0	48.86	
Theodore Roosevelt	1901	77.0	23.0	5.5	62.00	Henry Schroeder
Theresa	1877	52.5	21.0	3.5	24.68	Henry J. Ervin
Three Brothers	1861	57.0	20.0	4.0	37.29	
Traveler	1864	57.0	20.0	4.0	32.53	Jennings
Truckee	1867	76.00	32.0	6.0	147.95	Patrick H. Tiernan
Undine †	1902.	78.0	27.0	6.3	95.00	Hans Anderson
Verbena	1902	61.5	21.5	2.1	37.27	O. F. L. Farenkam
Veto	1876–				47.66	
Virginia	1891	76.0	25.5	3.5	54.92	William Munder
Volcano	1897	45.0	15.6	4.8	20.00	George W. Kneass
Wavelet †	1878	57.0	20.0	4.1	32.04	John J. Dirks
War Eagle	1865	58.2	20.0	4.0	33.54	
William	1861				55.00	Robinson
William and Albert †	1861	58.5	20.8	4.2	33.10	
Winfield Scott	1861	66.0	22.0	5.0	49.83	
Witch of the Bay	1870	44.0	20.0	3.0	22.45	
Wonder †	1868	62.0	23.0	5.0	49.15	
Yosemite	1874	54.0	17.6	4.5	28.48	William Munder
Young America	1859	51.0	15.0	3.0	23.92	

Photographs in Appendix
Courtesy National Maritime Museum,
San Francisco

Endnotes

Introduction

1. The most authoritative account of the development of American sailing ships is found in Howard I. Chapelle, *The History of American Sailing Ships* (New York, 1935), while a concise history of a less technical nature is found in Winthrop L. Marvin, *The American Merchant Marine, its History and Romance from 1620 to 1902* (New York, 1902); a more intensive treatment of specific periods is found in Arthur H. Clark, *The Clipper Ship Era* (New York, 1910), and in Basil Lubbock, *The Down Easters: American Deep-water Sailing Ships, 1869-1929* (Boston, 1929). For the most complete work dealing with smaller sailing vessels, see Howard I. Chapelle, *American Small Sailing Craft: Their Design, Development, and Construction* (New York, 1951).

I. Great Inland Sea: Early Navigation on San Francisco Bay

1. Frederick William Beechey, *Voyage to the Pacific* (London, 1831), vol. 2, 3-4.

2. Zoeth Skinner Eldredge, *The Beginnings of San Francisco* (San Francisco, 1912), 41, 42, 138 ff.

3. Louis Choris, *San Francisco One Hundred Years Ago, With Illustrations from Drawings made by Choris in the Year 1816 . . .*, trans. by Porter Garnett (San Francisco, 1913), facing iv.

4. John P. Young, *San Francisco, A History of the Pacific Coast Metropolis* (San Francisco, 1912), vol. 1, 37.

5. Felix Riesenberg, Jr., *Golden Gate, The Story of San Francisco Harbor* (New York, 1940), 38.

6. Eldredge, *Beginnings of San Francisco*, 210. The *Arroba* was equal to about 25 pounds.

7. Young, *San Francisco*.

8. Eldredge, *Beginnings of San Francisco*, 504.

9. William Heath Davis, *Sixty Years in California* (San Francisco, 1889), 8.

10. Richard Henry Dana, *Two Years Before the Mast* (New York, 1945), 237.

11. *Ibid.*, 239.

12. Young, *San Francisco*.

13. Frank Soulé, *Annals of San Francisco* (San Francisco, 1855), 163; Eldredge, *Beginnings of San Francisco*; Riesenberg, *Golden Gate*, 48; Young, *San Francisco*.

14. Davis, *Sixty Years*, 29 ff.

15. *Ibid.*, 15.

16. James Peter Zollinger, *Sutter: The Man and His Empire* (New York, 1939), 58.

17. Julian Dana, *The Sacramento, River of Gold* (New York, 1939), 74; Zollinger, *Sutter*, 99; Heinrich Lienhard, *A Pioneer at Sutter's Fort — 1846-50* (Los Angeles, 1941), 10.

18. Julian Dana, *The Sacramento*, 137.

19. Hubert Howe Bancroft, "Vessels on the California Coast, 1836-1845," MS., Bancroft Library, Berkeley. (This list is probably incomplete.)

20. Bancroft, *ibid.*, 26.

21. Bancroft, *ibid.*, 21.

22. *Alta California*, October 4, 1849.

23. United States Custom House, Port of San Francisco, "Coasting Licenses for Vessels under Twenty Tons, 1849-50," microfilm facsimiles in the Bancroft Library, Berkeley.

24. *California Star*, April 17, 1849.

25. Davis, *Sixty Years*, 149.

26. William Robinson Grimshaw, "His Narratives of Life & Events in California During 'Flush Times', particularly 1848-49," manuscript in the Bancroft Library, Berkeley.

27. *Alta California*, January 25, 1849.

28. "Coasting Licenses," U.S. Custom Records, Federal Archives, San Bruno.

29. *Alta California*, September 20, 1849; see also John Frederick Norse, *First History of Sacramento City* (first published in 1853; Sacramento, 1945), 30.

30. *Alta California*, August 2, 1849.

31. United States Custom House, Port of San Francisco, "Bills of Sale, 1851-53," microfilm facsimiles in the Bancroft Library, Berkeley.

II. San Francisco's Own Square-Toed Packets . . .

1. John Leale, *Recollections of a Tule Sailor* (San Francisco, 1939), 33.

2. "Henry Hall's Notes on the San Francisco Bay Scow Schooners," *The American Neptune*, I (1941), 87, 88.

3. United States Custom House, Port of San Francisco, "Coasting Licenses for Vessels under Twenty Tons, 1850," microfilm facsimiles in the Bancroft Library, Berkeley, California.

4. *Ibid.*

5. Howard I. Chapelle, *American Small Sailing Craft: Their Design, Development, and Construction* (New York, 1951), 45.

6. C. J. Klitgaard, "Fifty Years as a Master Mariner," *Ship's Bulletin* (Standard Oil Company of California; August, 1941), 17.

7. J. Porter Shaw, interviews, Oakland, California, March and April, 1952.

8. "Henry Hall's notes," *American Neptune*.

9. J. Porter Shaw said that scows, among other hastily procured craft went to Alaska during the rush. Other men who have knowledge of the activities of the scows, some newspaper references, and a few photographs attest that the scows often sailed beyond the Golden Gate, although it is probable that they did not engage in the general coastwise trade.

10. Chapelle, *American Sailing Craft*, 33.

11. Don Arques, interview, Sausalito, California, March 21, 1952.

12. Henry Hall, "The Shipbuilding Industry in the United States," *Tenth Census of the United States* (Washington, 1884).

13. United States Custom House, Port of San Francisco, "Master Carpenters' Certificates," Custom House, San Francisco. These documents, which boatbuilders filled out upon the completion of a vessel which was to be licensed, start in 1870 and list considerable information about each vessel.

14. H. L. Lorentzen, interview, San Rafael, California, March 10, 1952.

15. E. W. North ed., "Evolution of Shipping and Shipbuilding in California . . ., The Work of Patrick Henry Tiernan," *The Overland Monthly*, (1899), 143-153.

16. *Ibid.*

17. United States Custom House, "Master Carpenters' Certificates."

18. Roger R. Olmsted and Nancy Olmsted, *San Francisco Bayside* (San Francisco, 1981), 125-128.

19. Emil Munder, interviews, Mill Valley, California, March and April, 1952.

20. "Bills of Sale," from the collection in the San Francisco Maritime Museum.

21. Munder, interviews.

22. *Ibid.*

23. United States Department of Commerce, Bureau of Navigation, *Merchant Vessels of the United States . . . Year Ended June 30, 1925* (Washington, 1926).

24. Raymond Stone, interview, Petaluma, California, April 8, 1952. Stone owned the *Traveler* during the late 1930s.

25. H. C. Thomsen, interviews, San Francisco, July 21, 1954, and Redwood City, March 19, 1955.

26. George T. Smith, an old scow sailor and owner, estimated that there were 410 scows on the Bay in 1910 (interview in the Oakland *Tribune*, January 22, 1939). J. Porter Shaw, Emil Munder, Tom Crowley, and others familiar with the operations of the scows at this time generally agree on such an estimate. This high estimate should probably be accepted with caution; yet while there are no records available which list scow schooners as distinct from other types of schooners, the author has been able to identify more than 200 vessels as scow schooners, most of which were active around 1900-1910. As a large number certainly remain unidentified, 400 is not an incredible estimate, though 300 might be a safer one.

III. "Hay Scow" on the Bay

1. See title page and footnote 23 on page 95; J. Porter Shaw, interviews, Oakland, California, March and April, 1952; Emil Munder, interviews, Mill Valley, California, March and April, 1952; "Historic American Merchant Marine Survey, District #16, California, Report on Scow Schooners," transcript courtesy of Smithsonian Institution, Washington, D.C.

2. Old photographs. One of the best photographs of the hay wharf is in the collection of the Morton-Waters Co., 126 Sutter St., San Francisco. (Ed. note: Now part of the National Maritime Museum collections on the J. Porter Shaw Library.)

3. Captain Fred Klebingat, born in Kiel, Germany in 1889 died in Coos Bay, Oregon in 1985. The last fifteen years of his life were spent in close correspondence and fruitful interviews with Karl Kortum, Chief Curator of the National Maritime Museum at San Francisco, as Klebingat recalled details of his many voyages in square-rigged ships and schooners that sailed every ocean of the world. An omnivorous reader and creative researcher, Klebingat, for example, had annotated R. L. Stevenson's works as he sailed into ports earlier described in these classics. Klebingat made several trips to San Francisco's Channel Street area and described the Hay Wharf and scow schooner activity with Roger and Nancy Olmsted. His memory of San Francisco's turn-of-the-century waterfront was specific and detailed. Maritime history is far richer for Klebingat's recollections.

4. Nicholas P. Hardeman, *History of the Inland Seaport of Stockton, California*, Ph.D. dissertation, University of California, Berkeley, 1953.

5. "Daily Produce Receipts," *Alta California*, 1867, and San Francisco *Bulletin*, 1889. Daily lists of produce receipts were carried in many of the San Francisco newspapers at various times, and usually showed the names of the vessels arriving, the cargoes and consignees, together with periodical recapitulations of the receipts.

6. Horace Davis, "Wheat in California," *The Overland Monthly*, 2 (November, 1868), 445.

7. W. A. Starr, "Abraham Dubois Starr," *California Historical Society Quarterly*, 27 (September, 1948), 195.

8. Karl Kortum, "The Balclutha," (mimeographed publication of the San Francisco Maritime Museum, 1954), 3.

9. Caspar T. Hopkins and Joseph Ringot, *Shipbuilding on the Pacific Coast* (San Francisco, 1874), 6.

10. Kortum, "The Balclutha," 6.

11. Starr, "Abraham Dubois Starr," 197.

12. Photographs in the possession of the author shows this method of loading.

13. Jack Cavenaugh, interview, Cavenaugh Lumber Co., Petaluma, California, May 10, 1952.

14. Tom Crowley, interview, San Francisco, April 23, 1952. Walter Johnson, interview, Petaluma, California, April 26, 1952. Cavenaugh, interview.

15. Commercial Publishing Company, *Vessels Owned on the United States Pacific Coast and Hawaiian Islands* (San Francisco, 1900).

16. Johnson, interview.

17. Commercial Publishing Company, *Vessels Owned.*

18. United States Custom House, Port of San Francisco, "Master Carpenters' Certificates," Custom House, San Francisco.

19. Emil Munder, interviews, Mill Valley, California, March and April, 1952.

20. Margaret Ballard, *History of Coal Mining in the Mount Diablo Region, 1859-1885*, M.A. thesis, University of California, Berkeley, 1931.

21. John Leale, *Recollections of a Tule Sailor* (San Francisco, 1939), 46; "Daily Produce Receipts."

22. Ballard, *History of Coal Mining*, 57, 58.

23. Leale, *Recollections*, 33.

24. Old photographs in the possession of the San Francisco Maritime Museum show this procedure to have been very common.

25. Judson Farley, "Salt-making in Alameda," *The Overland Monthly*, VI (Feb., 1871), 106-111.

26. *Ibid.*; see also page   , Chapter V.

27. Otto Bortfeld, interview, San Rafael, California, May 10, 1952. Raymond H. Clarke, interviews, San Pablo Yacht Harbor, California, March 23, 1952. Both Bortfeld and Clarke operated scows in the sand and gravel business.

28. San Francisco *Examiner*, April 10, 1896.

29. Photograph in the collection of Allen Knight, Carmel, California.

30. Shaw, interviews.

IV. Master Mariner's Regatta

1. San Francisco *Bulletin*, July 5, 1867. The sources for this chapter, unless otherwise noted, were the San Francisco daily newspapers, for the Fourth of July and the days immediately preceding and following, from 1865 to 1900. The San Francisco *Chronicle* generally carried the most complete accounts of the regattas, and was therefore used the most extensively. In those cases when no accounts were available in the *Chronicle* - for example, before 1869 - or the stories in the *Chronicle* were poor, other newspapers were consulted. *The Bulletin, Call* and *Alta California* furnished stories of the races in 1867 and 1868, and the *Bulletin, Call* and San Francisco *Examiner* were used to fill out or check the *Chronicle* accounts of later years.

2. The sixth prize in the 1868 regatta, won by the scow *Rough and Ready*, was a fog horn and a pair of opera glasses.

3. The Master Mariners' Benevolent Association is still in existence and its meeting hall is decorated with a number of large paintings of the regattas and the more notable regatta winners; all other records of the regattas were lost in the 1906 fire.

4. Walter Johnson, interview, Petaluma, California, April 26, 1952.

5. United States Treasury Department, Bureau of Navigation, *Seventeenth Annual List of Merchant Vessels of the United States . . . For the Year Ended June 30, 1885* (Washington, 1885).

6. Raymond H. Clarke, interview, San Pablo Yacht Harbor, California, May 10, 1952; Clarke owned the *Rosella* around 1910.

Afterword: On the basis of a reprint of this chapter in *American West Magazine*, when Roger R. Olmsted was editor, Bill Vaughan and some yachting friends decided to revive the classic race in 1965. Vaughan was in charge of Maritime Day (traditionally every May), and he asked for the author's advice on the best way to revive the Master Mariner's Regatta for Maritime Day. As Vaughan remembers, "Essentially what he said was, 'Get the biggest goddamn boats you can get, put 'em in the race and try to attract the public by putting together a decent course that will allow people to see it.' "

"I put together the same format we have today," recalls Vaughan. "Yachts represent the working boats which used to participate in the regatta. The only way we could have historical continuity was to have the sponsors from the maritime industry — so that in essence, they were sailing on the vessel. It was their vessel for the day. Bill Ritter was instrumental in getting some old timers into it. And Larry Knight was of some assistance.... We had a guy by the name of Ray Bowes who was a member of the Master Mariner's Benevolent Association way back when.... Harry Dring was enthusiastic.... Jim Enzensperger was in with Pacific Far East Lines.... Robin Hobart took over the handicapping.... Everyone was enthusiastic. It rapidly became a sort of classic. One year we had *Serena, Charmain, Constellation* and *Astor* all racing.... When Bill Ritter died, I bought the *Billiken*, a real Master Mariner's vessel. Now I sail *Evening Star*, a yacht designed in 1936 by John Alden and built in 1937 by Herreshoff for Frederick Ford of the Detroit clan. *Evening Star* was first in the Class O Division of the Master Mariner's Regatta in 1974 and 1977. ... It's a real joy to see people like Hal Sommer who had the *Freda* and *Wanderbird*. Hal has done magnificent work restoring these fine vessels. I would like to see the Master Mariner's become a little more selective. I think it is important to encourage those with old boats and unique old-time rigs." *Latitude 38* Vol. 47, May, 1981.

V. Tule Sailors

1. San Francisco *Examiner*, November 11, 1917.

2. L. Hans Beck, interviews, San Mateo, California, February 26, March 5, March 19, 1955; unless otherwise cited, the material dealing with Beck comes from these interviews.

3. United States Custom House, Port of San Francisco, "Master Carpenters' Certificates," Custom House, San Francisco.

4. Tom Crowley, interview, San Francisco, April 23, 1952.

5. John Leale, *Recollections of a Tule Sailor* (San Francisco, 1939), 35.

6. Captain Fred Klebingat, oral history with Karl Kortum. Klebingat's memory of the Hay Wharf would date back to 1908, when he arrived in San Francisco.

7. Edward Morphy, "San Francisco's Thoroughfares." Typescript, 5 vols. San Francisco History Room, San Francisco Public Library.

8. Beck interviews; J. Porter Shaw, interviews, Oakland, California, March and April, 1952.

9. Beck, interviews.

10. Emil Munder, interviews, Mill Valley, California, March and April, 1952; H. C. Thomsen, interviews, San Francisco, July 21, 1954, and Redwood City, California, March 19, 1955. The material relating to the Jennings comes from these two sources, unless otherwise noted.

11. "Master Carpenters' Certificates."

12. Shaw, interviews.

13. W. H. Walls, interview, Petaluma, California, April 8, 1952.

14. Shaw, interviews.

15. Many photographs show this. Terms from *ibid.*

16. Crowley, interview; William Figari, interview, San Francisco, April 23, 1952.

17. Figari, interviews.

18. Oakland *Tribune*, November 15, 1936.

19. Crowley, interview.

20. Beck, interviews.

21. C. J. Klitgaard, "Fifty Years as a Master Mariner," *Ship's Bulletin*, (Standard Oil Company of California, August, 1941), 17.

22. Raymond Stone, interview, Petaluma, California, April 8, 1952.

23. *Ibid.*

24. *San Francisco Examiner*, August, 1896.

25. Jack McNairn, "Scow Schooner Sagas," *Sea and Pacific Motor Boat*, 47 (February, 1955), 78.

26. Shaw, interviews.

27. San Francisco *Call*, July 25, 1896.

28. Shaw, interviews.

VI. The Motor Scow

1. United States Custom House, Port of San Francisco, "Master Carpenters' Certificates," Custom House, San Francisco; Emil Munder, interviews, Mill Valley, March and April, 1952.

2. "Marine Engines," *The Rudder* (March, 1899), 123; Ernest W. Graef, "Types of Marine Motors," The *Rudder* (May, 1902), 259; J. Porter Shaw, interviews, Oakland, California, March and April, 1952.

3. "Marine Engines," 123.

4. Munder, interviews.

5. *Ibid.*

6. Several motor scows were lying around the shores of the bay in 1955: The *Annie L.* and *Matilda* at Alviso, *H. Eppinger, Albertine,* and *Grace and Amy* at the two Arques yards in Sausalito, *Gas Light* on the bank of Gallinas Creek, and *Hermine Blum* on a tule island across from Pittsburg were among those in the best state of preservation. The engines were still in some of these.

7. Petaluma *Argus*, June 9, 1914.

8. United States Department of Commerce, Bureau of Navigation, *Fifty-second Annual List of Merchant Vessels of the United States, for the Year Ended June 30, 1920* (Washington, 1920); see also the appendix. The figures quoted in this chapter as to the number of motor and sailing scows in operation at various times are based on the list in the appendix, which is certainly not 100% accurate, and may err most significantly in being incomplete. Thus, even in 1955, there may have been a few scows in operation which are not included in the appendix.

9. Don Arques, interview, Sausalito, Calif., March 21, 1952; L. Hans Beck, interviews, Feb. 26, March 5, March 19, 1955.

10. Raymond Stone, interview, April 8, 1952, Petaluma, California; also Arques and Munder, interviews.

11. "Master Carpenters' Certificates," *op. cit.*; as compared to United States Department of Commerce, Bureau of Navigation, *Merchant Vessels of the United States, Year Ended June 30, 1925* (Washington, 1926); also Munder, interviews.

12. Harold Anderson, interview, Redwood City, May, 1952. Mr. Anderson worked at Frank's Tannery at the time the *Grace & Amy* was built there.

13. United States Department of Commerce, *Fifty-second Annual List of Merchant Vessels*; and *Merchant Vessels*.

14. Pete Hanson, MS. statement in the San Francisco Maritime Museum "Log," November 17, 1951.

15. Arques, interview; also "Chart of Wrecks on the Pacific Coast," San Francisco Marine Exchange.

16. Raymond H. Clarke, interview, San Pablo Yacht Harbor, California. Clarke was operating the *Annie* when this incident occurred.

17. Arques and Shaw, interviews; *Fifty-second Annual List of Merchant Vessels.*

18. Hanson, MS. statement.

19. *Ibid.*, see note #6.

20. Stone, interview. Stone was engineer of the *Matilda*.

21. Stone, interview.

22. See note #6.

VII. Design & Construction of the San Francisco Bay Scow Schooner

1. United States Department of Commerce and Labor, Bureau of Navigation, *Thirty-ninth Annual List of Merchant Vessels of the United States . . . Year Ended June 30, 1907* (Washington, 1907).

    Lines of St. Thomas by J. Porter Shaw . . . The most authentic plans of a scow schooner presently known to exist are those of *St. Thomas*, made by Oakland lawyer and maritime antiquarian J. Porter Shaw (for whom the National Maritime Museum Library is named). Shaw seized the opportunity when the vessel was hauled out and on a ways to be converted to a barge to make his measurements. This was in the early 1920s and *St. Thomas* had never been motorized.

    On the other hand, the Historic American Merchant Marine Survey plans, made later, should be treated with a certain amount of caution. Photographs of the *Robbie Hunter*, for example, show that the vessel had more sheer than appears in the Survey drawings. This may be true of other schooners as well. The discrepancy may be because the vessels in the Survey were measured afloat, after losing a certain amount of their original shape — hogging would have probably taken place. Emil Munder, who built the *Crockett*, is described in the text as not remembering the deadrise that appears in the schooner's plans as drawn in the Historic American Merchant Marine Survey. (Notes by Karl Kortum, Chief Curator of the National Maritime Museum, San Francisco.

2. Photograph in the San Francisco Maritime Museum.

3. Howard I. Chapelle, *American Small Sailing Craft; Their Design, Development, and Construction* (New York, 1951), 33.

4. Don Arques, interview, Sausalito, Calif., March 21, 1952; Emil Munder, interviews, Mill Valley, Calif., March and April, 1952; J. Porter Shaw, interviews, Oakland, Calif., March and April, 1952.

5. *San Francisco Chronicle*, July 5, 1884, and July 5, 1885.

6. Munder, interviews.

7. Historic American Merchant Marine Survey, *Albertine*, Smithsonian Institution, Washington, survey 16-2, sheet 1. The hulk of the *Albertine* is now (1955) lying in Don Arques' boatyard in Sausalito, Calif.

8. Munder, interviews.

9. *Ibid.*

10. J. Porter Shaw, "midship section of the *Saint Thomas*," drawn about 1915, San Francisco Maritime Museum.

11. Munder, interviews.

12. *Ibid.*

13. Historic American Merchant Marine Survey, *Robbie Hunter*, Smithsonian Institution, Washington, D.C., survey 16-7, sheet 1.

14. Chapelle, *American Small Sailing Craft*, 51.

15. Historic American Merchant Marine Survey, *Mary*, Smithsonian Institution, Washington, D.C., survey 16-8, sheet 1.

16. Historic American Merchant Marine Survey, District #16, California, "Report on Scow Schooners," transcript courtesy of the Smithsonian Institution, Washington, p. 1.

17. Munder, interviews. Karl Kortum notes: Edge bolting the planks again must have presented difficulties.

18. "Report on Scow Schooners."

19. Shaw, interviews.

20. Munder, interviews.

21. Chapelle, *American Small Sailing Craft*, 70.

22. Munder, interviews.

23. Arques, interviews. Robert J. Cleek adds these notes on distinctive characteristics of scow rigs: "(1) The bowsprit was sometimes 'fiddled' with at the butt to allow it to be run inboard and out of the way for berthing alongside and for handling cargo when run ashore by the bow. (2) Scows were reefed not only in the normal way, by shortening the sail from the top down, lowering the gaffboom and tying reef points at the mainboom, as with any gaffer, but also by 'reefing up' with the mainboom higher and the gaffboom topped, so that the mainboom cleared the characteristically high deckloads. (3) The most characteristic detail of scow schooner rigged was the manner in which the main topsail was furled and brailed. The main topsails were apparently not set 'flying,' being raised from the deck when used but were kept aloft and gathered in at the topmast when not in use. (4) The steering gear was peculiar to scows. The outboard hung 'barn door' rudders were swung not from a tiller in the rudderpost, but with the tail of a purchase attached to a T-bar on the after top edge of the rudder. The standing part was fastened to the stern with the running part led *through* distinctive holes or ports in the transom. That running part was then led to the wheel drum. This unique movable steering assembly could be raised quite high so the helmsman could have a clear view over the deckload."

VIII. *Alma* Sails Again!

1. Roy Peterson interview, March 29, 1974. Tape at J. Porter Shaw Library, National Maritime Museum, San Francisco.

2. Olga Peterson Likens notes on photograph, recorded by Karl Kortum, National Maritime Museum, San Francisco.

3. Roger Olmsted, notes.

4. Harry Dring interviewed by Barbara Fetesoff, April 1974.

5. Peterson interview.

6. Barbara J. Fetesoff, "The Scow Schooner *Alma*, 1891-1975," M.A. thesis, San Jose State University, February 1975, pp. 44-48.

7. Peterson interview.

8. United States Federal Archives, San Bruno, "Wreck Reports."

9. Fetesoff, "Scow Schooner *Alma*," p. 15.

10. Peter John Gametta interview by Barbara Fetesoff, January 5, 1975. Tape at J. Porter Shaw Library, National Maritime Museum, San Francisco.

11. *Ibid.*

12. Fetesoff, "Scow Schooner *Alma*," pp. 22-23.

13. Roger Olmsted notes.

14. Karl Kortum letter to Scott Newhall, editor of *San Francisco Chronicle*, March 5, 1949.

15. Karl Kortum notes, "The Saving of *Alma*." National Maritime Museum, San Francisco.

16. Correspondence between Harry Dring and Robert E. Stewart, Supervisor, Mt. Diablo State Park, August 22, 1959.

17. Harry Dring interviews by Barbara J. Fetesoff, May 23 and December 11, 1974.

18. Fetesoff, "Scow Schooner *Alma*," p. 30.

19. *Ibid.*, pp. 32-33.

20. Correspondence between Harry Dring and David Redding, Manager, San Mateo Coast Area, California State Parks, May 26, 1969.

Bibliography

Bibliographical note:

One of the most useful documentary sources to the American maritime historian is the annual abstract of current registers and enrollments of vessels published by the United States Government Printing Office. This volume has been issued as of June 30 for each year since 1867, excepting 1869 and 1877, through 1939; since 1940 it has been issued as of January 1. The agency preparing the volume has changed several times during the last seventy-five years: through 1883, it was compiled by the Treasury Department, Bureau of Statistics; from 1884-1902 by the Treasury Department, Bureau of Navigation; from 1903-1912 by the Department of Commerce and Labor, Bureau of Navigation; from 1913-1932 by the Department of Commerce, Bureau of Navigation; from 1932-1935 by the Department of Commerce, Bureau of Navigation and Steamboat Inspection; from 1936-1942 by the Department of Commerce, Bureau of Marine Inspection and Navigation; and since 1943 by the Treasury Department, Bureau of Customs.

Through the first seven issues this source was titled *Mercantile Navy of the United States*; the 1875 edition was called *Eighth Annual List of Merchant Vessels of the United States*, and this title-scheme was continued through the *Fifty-Sixth Annual List*, in 1924; with the 1925 edition, the title became *Merchant Vessels of the United States*. Important additions to the information given about each vessel came in 1884, when net tonnage and when and where built were added; dimensions of rigged vessels have appeared since 1885, and the name and address of the managing owner since 1925. Those used most extensively in this work are cited with the notes for each chapter, and are the editions of 1885 (the first with dimensions of vessels), 1907 (after the construction of the last sailing scow), 1920, and 1925.

Unprinted Material

Ballard, Margaret. "History of Coal Mining in the Mount Diablo Region, 1854-1885," M.A. thesis, University of California, Berkeley, 1931.

Bancroft, Hubert Howe, "Vessels on the California Coast, 1836-1845." MS., Bancroft Library, Berkeley.

Cleaveland, Alice Mae. "The North Bay Shore During the Spanish and Mexican Regimes." M.A. thesis, University of California, Berkeley, 1933.

Fetesoff, Barbara Joyce. "The Scow Schooner *Alma*, 1891-1975," M.A. thesis, San Jose State University, San Jose, 1975.

Grimshaw, William Robinson, "His Narrative of Life & Events in California During 'Flush Times', particularly 1848-49," MS, Bancroft Library.

Hall Brothers. "No. 122, Mr. Rowe's Scow Schooner." Draught in the San Francisco Maritime Museum collection.

Hanson, Pete. MS. statement in the San Francisco Maritime Museum. "Log." November 17, 1951.

Hardeman, Nicholas Perkins. "The Historical Background of the Deepwater Port at Stockton, 1850-1927." M.A. thesis, University of California, Berkeley, 1950.

Hardeman, Nicholas Perkins. "History of the Inland Seaport of Stockton, California." Ph.D. dissertation, University of California, Berkeley, 1953.

Hill, F. G. "Place of the Grain Trade in California Economic Development, 1870-1900," mimeographed by F. G. Hill, University of California, Berkeley, 1954.

Historic American Merchant Marine Survey. *Albertine*. Smithsonian Institution, Washington, survey 16-2, sheet 1.

Historic American Merchant Marine Survey. *Crockett*. Smithsonian Institution, Washington, survey 16-1, sheet 1.

Historic American Merchant Marine Survey. *Mary*. Smithsonian Institution, Washington, survey 16-8, sheet 1.

Historic American Merchant Marine Survey. *Robbie Hunter*. Smithsonian Institution, Washington, survey 16-7, sheet 1.

Historic American Merchant Marine Survey. District #16, California. "Report on Scow Schooners." Transcript courtesy of the Smithsonian Institution, Washington.

Johnson, William David. "Inland Steam Navigation in California." M.A. thesis, Stanford University, 1952.

Kortum, Karl. "The Life and Times of the Ship Balclutha." Mimeographed by the San Francisco Maritime Museum, 1954.

McGowan, Joseph Aloysius. "San Francisco-Sacramento Shipping: 1839-1854." M.A. thesis, University of California, Berkeley, 1939.

Marten, Effie El Freda. "Development of Wheat Culture in the San Joaquin Valley, 1846-1900." M.A. thesis, University of California, Berkeley, 1925.

Pattijohn, Lucy. "Development of the San Francisco Waterfront." M.A. thesis, University of California, Berkeley, 1927.

Pivernetz, Joseph Albert. "An Economic Survey of the Industrial Development of Crockett, California." M.A. thesis, University of California, 1931.

South, Arethuse Aurelia. "California Inland Navigation: 1839-1890." M.A. thesis, University of California, 1939.

Teese, Edith. "Waterfront Developments in the San Pablo and Richmond, California, region to 1917." M.A. thesis, University of California, Berkeley, 1947.

Treutlein, Theodore Edward. "Early Exploration of San Francisco Bay." M.A. thesis, University of California, Berkeley, 1930.

United States Custom House, Port of San Francisco. "Bills of Sale, 1851-1853." Microfilm facsimiles in Bancroft Library, Berkeley.

United States Custom House, Port of San Francisco. "Coasting Licenses for Vessels under Twenty Tons, 1849-1840." Microfilm, Bancroft Library.

United States Custom House, Port of San Francisco. "Master Carpenters' Certificates." Custom House, San Francisco.

"Vessels Lost on the Pacific Coast." Chart, San Francisco Marine Exchange.

Voget, Lamberta Margarette. "The Waterfront of San Francisco, 1863-1930." Ph.D. dissertation, University of California, Berkeley, 1943.

Woodruff, Jacqueline McCart. "History of Benicia, 1846-1880." M.A. thesis, University of California, Berkeley, 1946.

Yates, John. "Sketch of a Journey in 1842 through Sacramento Valley." MS., Bancroft Library, Berkeley.

Newspapers

Alta California (San Francisco).

California Star (San Francisco).

Oakland *Tribune*.

Petaluma *Argus*.

San Francisco *Bulletin*.

San Francisco *Call*.

San Francisco *Chronicle*.

San Francisco *Examiner*.

Note: the exact titles of some of these newspapers changed slightly during the period 1849-1915 (e.g., *Daily Evening Bulletin*); the title cited above is the usual title by which the newspaper has been known.

Books, Booklets, and Periodical Literature

"Accurate California Statistics," *Land of Sunshine*, 14 (January, February, 1901), 53-54, 135-136: 15 (July, 1901), 49.

Bancroft, Hubert Howe. *History of California*. 7 vols. San Francisco, 1884-1890.

Beechey, Frederick Wilhelm. *Voyage to the Pacific*. 2 vols. London, 1821.

Brown, Colvin B. "San Joaquin County and Stockton, the Gateway City," *Land of Sunshine*, 15 (July, 1901), 91-108.

Burgess, Sherwood D. "The Forgotten Redwoods of the East Bay," California Historical Society *Quarterly*, 30 (March, 1951), 1-14.

Buttner, L. N. "Port Costa: California's Grain Depot." *Sunset*, 4 (January, 1900), 104-106.

Camp, William Martin. *San Francisco: Port of Gold*. New York, 1947.

Chapelle, Howard I. *American Small Sailing Craft: Their Design, Development, and Construction*. New York, 1951.

Chapelle, Howard I. *The History of American Sailing Ships*. New York, 1935.

Choris, Louis. *San Francisco One Hundred Years Ago, With Illustrations from Drawings made by Choris in the Year 1816, . . .* Trans. by Porter Garnett. San Francisco, 1913.

Clark, Arthur H. *The Clipper Ship Era*. New York, 1910.

Commercial Publishing Company. *Vessels Owned on the United States Pacific Coast and Hawaiian Islands*. San Francisco, 1900.

Dana, Julian. *The Sacramento, River of Gold*. New York, 1939.

Dana, Richard Henry. *Two Years Before the Mast*. New York, 1945.

Davis, Horace. "California Breadstuffs." *Journal of Political Economy*, 2 (September, 1894), 526 ff.

Davis, Horace. "Wheat in California." *The Overland Monthly*, 1 (November, 1868), 442-452.

David, William Heath. *Sixty Years in California*. San Francisco, 1889.

Eldredge, Zeoth Skinner. *The Beginnings of San Francisco*. San Francisco, 1912.

Farley, Judson. "Salt Making in Alameda." *The Overland Monthly*, 6 (February, 1871), 105-112.

Final Report of the Senate Fact-finding Committee on San Francisco Bay Ports, Sacramento, 1951.

Francis, Philip. "A Pacific Granery." *Sunset*, 2 (March, 1890), 90-94.

"Freighting on San Francisco Bay." *Pacific Motor Boat* (March, 1937).

Graef, Ernest W. "Types of Marine Motors." *The Rudder* (May, 1901), 259.

Hall, Henry. *Shipbuilding Industry in the United States. Tenth Census of the United States*. Washington, 1884.

Harlan, George H., and Clement Fisher, Jr. *Of Walking Beams and Paddle Wheels*. San Francisco, 1951.

"Henry Hall's Notes on the San Francisco Bay Scow Schooners." *The American Neptune*, 1 (1941), 87, 88.

Hopkins, Caspar Thomas, and Joseph Ringot. *Ship Building on the Pacific Coast*. San Francisco, 1867.

Hopkins, Caspar Thomas, and Joseph Ringot. *Shipbuilding on the Pacific Coast*. San Francisco, 1874.

Hopkins, Caspar Thomas, with Geo. C. Perkins, Andrew Crawford, *et al*. *Report on Port Charges, Shipping and Ship-building to the Manufacturers Association, the Board of Trade, and the Chamber of Commerce of San Francisco*. San Francisco, 1885.

Klitgaard, C. J. "Fifty Years as a Master Mariner." *Ship's Bulletin* (Standard Oil Company of California; July and August, 1941), 17, 18.

Leale, John. *Recollections of a Tule Sailor*. San Francisco, 1939.

Lienhard, Heinrich. *A Pioneer at Sutter's Fort — 1846-50*. Trans. and ed. by Marguerite Eyer Wilbur. Los Angeles, 1941.

Lubbock, Basil. *The Down Easters: American Deep-water Sailing Ships, 1869-1927*. Boston, 1929.

Lyman, John. "Pacific Coast-built Sailers." *Marine Digest*, (16 August, 1941), 2 ff.; (13 September, 1941), 2 ff.

Lyman, John. *The Sailing Vessels of the Pacific Coast and Their Builders: 1850-1905*. Maritime Research Society of San Diego Bulletin #2 (reprinted from *Americana*, 35, April, 1941).

Macarthur, Walter. *Last Days of Sail on the Pacific Coast*. San Francisco, 1929.

MacMullen, Jerry. *Paddle-Wheel Days in California*. Stanford University, 1944.

McNairn, Jack. "Scow Schooner Sagas." *Sea and Pacific Motor Boat*, 47 (February, 1955). 7, 8, 66, 76-79.

"Marine Engines." *The Rudder* (March, 1899), 123.

Marvin, Winthrop L. *The American Merchant Marine, its History and Romance from 1620 to 1902*. New York, 1902.

Mears, Eliot G. *Maritime Trade of the Western United States*. Stanford, 1935.

Morse, John Frederick. *First History of Sacramento City*. 1853 Sacramento, 1945.

North, E. M. ed. "Evolution of Shipping and Shipbuilding in California. . . . . The Work of Patrick Henry Tiernan." *The Overland Monthly* 33 (1899), 143-153.

Olmsted, Roger R. and Nancy, *Rincon de las Salinas y Potero Viejo*, San Francisco, 1979.

Olmsted, Roger R. and Nancy, *San Francisco Bayside*, San Francisco, 1981.

Olmsted, Roger R. and Nancy, *The San Francisco Waterfront*, San Francisco, 1976.

Riesenberg, Felix, Jr. *Golden Gate: the Story of San Francisco Harbor.* New York, 1940.

Ringgold, Commander Cadawaller. *A Series of Charts with Sailing Directions Embracing Surveys of the Farallones, Entrance to the Bay of San Francisco, Bay of San Francisco and San Pablo, Straits of Carquinez and Suisun Bay, Confluence and Delta Branches of the Sacramento River . . . to the American River, including the Cities of Sacramento and Boston, State of California.* Washington, 1851.

Rowe, William Hutchinson. *The Maritime History of Maine: Three Centuries of Shipbuilding and Seafaring.* New York, 1948.

Soulé, Frank. *Annals of San Francisco.* San Francisco, 1885.

Starr, W. A. "Abraham Dubois Starr: Pioneer California Miller and Wheat Exporter." California Historical Society *Quarterly*, 27 (September, 1948), 193-202.

Young, John P. *San Francisco, A History of the Pacific Coast Metropolis.* 2 vols. San Francisco, 1912.

Zollinger, Janes Peter. *Sutter: The Man and His Empire.* New York, 1939.

Wonder *Awaits the Breeze . . . Quiet afternoon on San Francisco Bay at the turn of the century. Full load of cargo and not much wind to fill her sails. Plenty of time to have a smoke and swap stories. Many a seagoing man envied the simple, independent life of a scow schooner man.*

National Maritime Museum, San Francisco

Index

Back cover

Quiet Reflections on the Sacramento . . . *Scow schooner men passed many pleasant days up the rivers. They often had time for some fishing or duck hunting and some married men took their wives along once or twice a year on a river run. Friendly farmers sometimes offered a country meal. And sometimes a light fingered scow man would jump ashore and "hook a couple of watermelons and then jump aboard the next time the vessel came about on that side of the river."*

National Maritime Museum
San Francisco